MW01677685

Battleship SCHARNHORST

Gerhard Koop
Klaus-Peter Schmolke

CONWAY
MARITIME PRESS

Jacket illustrations:
Front: *Scharnhorst* in 1939 in the Forth of Kiel.
A 1:100 scale model of *Scharnhorst* in the Kuesten-museum, Wilhelmshaven.
Back: Internal profile and deck plan.

Copyright © Conway Maritime Press, 1998

First published in Germany as 'Vom Originale zum modell: Schlatschiff *Scharnhorst*'

First published in Britain by
Conway Maritime Press,
a division of Batsford Communications PLC,
583 Fulham Road
LONDON SW6 5BY

This edition specially published for
The Military Book Club,
Doubleday Direct,
1540 Broadway,
New York, NY 10036

ISBN 0-85177-772-4

All rights reserved. Unauthorised duplication contravenes applicable laws.

Translated by Lt Col Bernd E P Rolff
Designed by Simon Ray-Hills
Printed in Hong Kong

Contents

Preface

This publication mainly covers the battleship* *Scharnhorst*, although much of the data is compared with that of her sister ship *Gneisenau*. It contains the most important technical information along with a brief general history of shipbuilding and a description of ship construction. There are additional notes on life on board, crew training and the various states of readiness. There are numerous photographs of both the original ship and a variety of models, which are complemented by illustrations of *Gneisenau* to demonstrate the vital differences between these two sister ships. This collection of data, specifications, photographs and line drawings provides the modeller with all essential information on his chosen subject, and directs him to further sources of research material. Some of the general information contained within this title may refer to other units of the same class but only when these are similar to the ship covered by the appropriate book. All the plans within these pages are smaller scale renderings of those contained in an original 'Planrolle' (set of drawings) which accompanied the first German edition of the book.

I wish to express my special thanks to Mr Klaus-Peter Schmolke, who made all the excellent drawings, and Mr F Bavendamm, who took all the photographs of the model. I also wish to express my gratitude to the Kuestenmuseum, Wilhelmshaven for their kind permission for photographs to be taken of the models in their museum.

Gerhard Koop

* **Note: Although the British always referred to these ships as battlecruisers on account of their high speed and comparatively lighter guns, the German Navy always referred to them as battleships.**

Shipbuilding

As with the construction of a real ship, the modeller has to obey certain principles. If he wants to build a model which is not true to life then it is entirely up to him how to build it. There are plenty of these models around, and most were the result of a simple inspiration. In most cases, however, the modeller strives to build a model which is as close to the original as possible.

In former times – the times of the sailing ships – modelmakers (mainly sailors) had plenty of time to build their models as their ship's journey lasted many months. They also could constantly refer to the original working ship. If it was a simple static model or a ship in a bottle then only the exterior of the ship had to be modelled, but if a floating model was wanted things became more complicated as other factors, including stability, had also to be taken into consideration.

Until the beginning of the nineteenth century shipbuilding was not ruled by any strict guidelines: it was the responsibility of the individual shipwrights to decide how a vessel should be designed and constructed. These shipwrights had very good reputations, although a great deal of their individual 'traditions' had much to do with guesswork and knowledge of past successes. The customer could make specific demands when placing an order for a vessel including the number of guns, or ship's complement, when a warship was required.

A uniform method of shipbuilding began to be developed by the seventeenth century when a simple classification system was introduced with the number of guns determining the type, eg 70-gun ship, and became standard. Despite this, the appearance of individual ships within the same 'type' differed considerably. By the mid-nineteenth century these uniform types were sub-divided into classes. Ships belonging to the same class were from then on more or less identical as far as dimensions, weight, armament and equipment were concerned.

The task for today's model shipwright, however, is an easier one, and there are plenty of plans and instructions available telling him how to build the model. These plans are reconstructions of the originals, and there is hardly anything the modeller can do wrong. It is up to him, with regard to the skills he possesses, how he is to complete the model: as a static display model or as a floating model.

The construction of a ship

In the beginning, there is a staff requirement containing all the components of the desired warship: size, armament, armour, speed and endurance. These are based on tactical considerations such as mission of the ship, her ability to overcome opponents and the ability to evade a superior adversary. These operational considerations are forwarded to the design office, where the first sketch designs are drafted. These designs are then submitted to other departments until a consensus is achieved. The result of this is a draft which shows the appearance, the compartments, and the arrangement of the armament and armour. This includes weight calculations, so that it is then possible to make detailed calculations and develop them for working design. Marine-Oberbaurat Blechschmidt were responsible for the development of *Scharnhorst*.

The single criteria for the development and construction of a warship is summed up as battleworthiness. This is the sum of all built-in features, such as combat power, speed and manoeuverability, along with the training of the crew and leadership. In other words, it is the sum of weights of the ship's hull, machinery, armament, armour and other equipment combined with the other factors that cannot be precisely calculated.

Combat power consists of the two components 'combat effectiveness' and 'survivability'. 'Combat effectiveness' means the number of guns, their calibres, muzzle energy, ranges and rate of fire, but also the training of the crew and effective fire control systems. Additionally, the ship needs to be seaworthy and provide a stable platform for her guns, even in the roughest seas, so that her armament can remain operational. Lighter weapons can be stabilised, but that is not possible with the secondary or main guns. 'Survivability' includes armour protection, pumping arrangements and flooding valves, fire protection, watertight compartments, the arrangement of main and auxiliary engines, and also stability and buoyancy.

Speed is a factor essential for the operational capability of the ship. She must be able to change speed and course rapidly.

Endurance is the term used to describe the length of time a ship can stay at sea, sometimes referred to as range.

To sum up, every requirement at the beginning of the design process of a ship is a demand for the maximum. The operational department demands a ship which combines all the factors mentioned, while the gunners demand a calibre as large as possible and as many guns as possible. Other departments ask for heavy armour protection, and the ship also has to be as fast as possible with a maximum range.

All this, of course, cannot be achieved in one single design. A large-calibre armament requires a large ship and if extensive armour protection is required, the ship will have to be larger still. In order to provide such a super-ship with high speed and a maximum range, powerful machinery will have to be installed, which again requires more space. Within a hull of a given size, additional armour and armament can only be installed at the expense of machinery, and this means reduced speed and range. If a certain speed and range are to be maintained, then armament and armour will have to be reduced. Consequently, the building of every warship is a compromise, which must be settled before completion of the final set of drawings, and only then can the ship be built.

Crew training

As early as possible during construction, members of the future ship's company begin to assemble. Many of these are members of the engine room staff who supervise the installation of the machinery they will later operate with its pipes, tubes, leads etc, and get acquainted with it. In the meantime, other specialized personnel are sent on instruction courses run by the manufacturers of boilers, turbines, shafts, bearings, pumps, diesel engines for powerplants, generators, gyro compasses etc.

This first phase of training is concluded once the crew is complete and the ship has been commissioned. After the crew has been organised into divisions and watches full training begins, the aim of which is close cooperation. This training starts with guided tours through the ship to make the layout familiar. After this the newly-posted sailors, who, when they joined, had only received basic training or specialized training in their area of expertise, will all be able to work together as a team.

Manning the action stations

General knowledge of the ship has to be extensive, and this applies particularly to all personnel employed in the engine rooms. It is essential that they know their stations, even in the dark; they must know where every valve, shutter and stop valve is, even with the station pitch-black. Differently shaped handles on the various elements make this task somewhat easier. All pipes in each compartment are marked by coloured bands. Each colour has a different meaning, with leads, cables and cable runs marked accordingly.

Closely related to the *Schiffskunde* 'general knowledge of the ship' is the *Rollendienst* 'stations drill' which, at the beginning, is conducted in the harbour.

The sailor learns to man important stations during alerts such as 'fire in the ship', 'man overboard', 'air attack imminent', and will learn everything about the ship's various states of readiness. This station drill will be repeated many times during the first trials of the ship, reaching its peak in the *Gefechtsdrill* 'action drill'. The first section of this training on board is concluded by a muster conducted by the ship's captain. Next there comes a transitory phase *Gefechtsausbildung* 'action training' which includes instruction in troubleshooting and battle-practice. The crew is also trained in the art of repairing the ship and her machinery in preparation for battle damage, and the final step is a muster under battle conditions. The training, however, is by no means finished; stations drill and action drill will be continued as long as the ship is commissioned. A permanent aid for all members of the crew is the *Rollenkarte* 'station card' which is always to be carried and serves as a guide and a memory aid on board. The *Rollen* consists of plans which tell every member of the crew what to do and where to do it. It also contains the personal number allocated to every member of the ship's company, and this number is the key for the appropriate affiliation to a certain division, watch or action station. It also tells which responsibilities the individual has within an action station.

The ship's watertight subdivision

There are many different states of a warship's subdivision. Many of these are allocated to a particular state of readiness, but different higher or lower states can always be ordered.

Doors, hatches, scuttles, manholes, sounding pipes, and other openings for various purposes all come under the collective term *Verschluesse* 'openings'. Whenever danger is imminent the ship can be protected by closing some, or all, of these openings as a preventative measure. The state of this preventative measure is based on the level of the possible, or present, threat. At sea, a higher degree of safety is required than in harbour, and journeys in fog or dangerous waters will require a higher state of safety than a journey in the open sea. The highest state of watertight subdivision is required when there is danger imminent or the ship is in action.

There are schedules for the various states of the ship's subdivision.

Normaler Verschlusszustand 'normal state of watertight subdivision': This is a standing order, and all other doors and hatches which may remain open under certain conditions, such as side scuttles in harbour, will be covered by special orders. All deviations from the ordered normal state, such as the opening of bunker hatches, may only be temporarily carried out for work. All openings in this state bear no special markings and include, for example, store rooms, sounding pipes, and bunker hatches. They usually remain closed at all times and may only be opened for particular tasks and only by assigned members of the crew. All other openings are specially marked with a red band.

Verschaerfter Verschlusszustand 'stringent state of watertight subdivision': This order will be given on special occasions such as exercises and navigating in fog or storms. Under this state only certain doors are allowed to remain open or are allowed to be opened for passage. All these special doors are marked with a red ball within a red band. Upon the order *Schotten dicht* 'close all watertight doors', these doors, too, will be closed, and may only be opened temporarily for access.

Klarschiffverschlusszustand 'action state of watertight subdivision': This is the state established according to the regulations for the manning of action stations. All openings which are allowed to remain open bear special markings. All members of the crew are responsible for sealing the ship once the order 'close all watertight doors' is given, and this order means all openings marked with the red ball. Upon action readiness only those openings necessary for the employment of the ship's armament may remain open, all others may only be temporarily opened for passage. All openings locked upon the order 'close all watertight doors' may only be opened with the permission of damage control.

As a rule, a higher state of watertight integrity automatically includes the previous lower state.

States of readiness

Like the various states of the ship's subdivision, there are also certain states of readiness for the crew, which are ordered as necessary.

'Harbour stations': normal harbour duties.

'Harbour action stations': normal harbour duties, but wartime watches have been alerted, AA guns manned etc, and the appropriate state of the ship's subdivision has been established.

'Cruising stations': normal duties at sea with the appropriate state of the ship's subdivision established.

'Second state of readiness': duties at sea with higher state of readiness, all weapons manned and appropriate state of the ship's subdivision established. There are three different types of the second state of readiness, mainly affecting the machinery.

'Action stations': the highest state of readiness, all weapons manned, all damage control parties and fire parties alerted. The machinery is ready to provide maximum power. All states of readiness were announced over the ship's public address system, with alarm bells ringing. On large ships such as *Scharnhorst* and *Gneisenau* – at least in the early days of their careers – a drummer and a bugler also sounded the alert by touring the whole ship and rousing the crew.

Engine room combat readiness

This particular state of readiness affected the ship's main engines and the boilers, including auxiliary machinery. The main task of engine room combat readiness is the maintenance or repair of the main machinery and the power supply. The German Navy's official regulations for engine room combat readiness were laid down in the *Anleitung für den Maschinengefechtsdienst* (MGDA), volume 1 - M Dv. Nr 412 (secret) dated 19 August 1938.

In case of hits or severe damage which could be detrimental to the ship there were a number of measures.

- Maintenance of the buoyancy of the ship as a prerequisite of all other measures.
- Avoidance of a total failure of the power supply for damage control (pumps, valves, fire fighting).
- Avoidance of a total failure of the main machinery.
- Maintenance of combat readiness of the armament.
- Repair of any element of the ship's damage control, power supply and armament that has failed.

The following table is an extract from the German *Kriegsmarine* (navy) regulations, showing the watch system in effect under action conditions

With the exception of the ship's leading personnel and the engine room personnel, the rest of the crew such as the gunners did not have to do any extra watch duties. In the engine room, however, there was always a full watch system with three watches. Under normal circumstances two of these watches were off-duty but could still be used to undertake repairs when necessary. Under action conditions the first watch would supply the personnel for the *Maschinenstoerungsabwehr* 'engine failure defence' under the command of the engineer officer and the officer in charge of electrical engineering, who would employ them in case of losses. The petty officers and junior ratings of the first watch would man their action stations according to the prescribed drill. The engine room personnel consisted of engine room groups, powerplant groups, repair parties, cutting and welding parties, runners, and couriers. The pump master with his personnel and the off-duty watch manned the damage control under the command of the ship's executive officer and the damage control officer.

Meals were usually taken at action stations, normally during lulls in fighting.

Beispiel einer Kriegswachverteilung der technischen Divisionen bei 3-Wachablösung (Kriegsmarsch)

Wache 8—12		
00.00 00.45	3/4 h	Waschen, Umziehen
00.45 04.45	4 h	**Leckwehr 4**
04.45 07.00	2 1/4 h	**Ruhe**
07.00 07.45	3/4 h	Waschen, Frühstück Klarmachen zur Wache
07.45 11.45	4 h	**Seewache 1**
11.45 12.45	1 h	Waschen, Umziehen Mittagessen
12.45 16.45	4 h	**Leckwehr 1**
16.45 17.00	1/4 h	Kaffeeausgabe
17.00 19.00	2 h	**Ruhe**
19.00 19.45	3/4 h	Waschen, Abendessen Klarmachen zur Wache
19.45 24.00	4 1/4 h	**Seewache 4**

Wache 12—4		
00.00 04.00	4 h	**Seewache 5**
04.00 04.45	3/4 h	Waschen, Umziehen
04.45 08.45	4 h	**Leckwehr 5**
08.45 09.00	1/4 h	Waschen, Frühstück
00.00 11.00	2 h	**Ruhe**
11.00 11.45	3/4 h	Waschen, Mittagessen Klarmachen zur Wache
11.45 15.45	4 h	**Seewache 2**
15.45 16.45	1 h	Waschen, Umziehen Kaffeeausgabe
16.45 20.45	4 h	**Leckwehr 2**
20.45 21.15	1/2 h	Waschen, Abendessen
21.15 23.45	2 1/2 h	**Ruhe**
23.45 24.00	1/4 h	Waschen Klarmachen zur Wache

Wache 4—8		
00.45 03.45	3 h	**Ruhe**
03.45 04.00	1/4 h	Wecken Klarmachen zur Wache
04.00 07.45	3 3/4 h	**Seewache 6**
07.45 08.45	1 h	Waschen, Umziehen Frühstück
08.45 12.45	4 h	**Leckwehr 6**
12.45 13.30	3/4 h	Waschen, Mittagessen
13.30 15.30	2 h	**Ruhe**
15.30 15.45	1/4 h	Wecken Klarmachen zur Wache
15.45 19.45	4 h	**Seewache 3**
19.45 20.45	1 h	Waschen, Umziehen, Abendessen
20.45 00.45	4 h	**Leckwehr 3**

Extract from the *Anleitung für den Maschinengefechtsdienst* (regulations for engine room combat readiness) (MGDA), volume 1 - M Dv Nr 412 (secret) dated 19 August 1938, published by the OKM (supreme command of the navy).

7 Various states of engine room combat readiness

The division of personnel for one of the following states of readiness for action conditions were ordered by the ship's captain. The aim of this measure was not only to relieve the personnel from excessive strain but also to save fuel. The various states of readiness were directly related to the number of boilers and engines, and the power supply, that had to be kept operational.

Kriegsmarschzustand 3 'Action condition 3'
Action basic switching (engine room division): limited operation of all plants and installations (power supply, fresh water supply, oil filters and pumps according to demand); basic switching for lighting, ventilation, communications, rudders and searchlights. In this state, it took some 60 minutes to get the ship ready for action.

Kriegsmarschzustand 2 'Action condition 2'
Action basic switching (engine room division); within the separate engine rooms, all necessary machines operating; auxiliary machinery according to demand; all powerplants working; all necessary generators and transformers operating to supply sufficient power for lighting, ventilation, communication, rudders and searchlights. In this state, it took some 30 minutes to get the ship ready for action.

Kriegsmarschzustand 1 'Action condition 1'
Action basic switching (engine room division); within the separate engine rooms, all necessary machines operating to provide sufficient power for the state of action condition ordered; all other units on stand-by (boilers lit and under pressure, engines pre-heated, all units ready to start); auxiliary machinery according to demand; all powerplants working; all necessary generators and transformers operating to supply sufficient power for lighting, ventilation, communication, rudders and searchlights; all other units on stand-by (generators idling, ready for operation). In this state, it took some 10 minutes to get the ship ready for action.

'Ship ready for action': Action basic switching; all systems necessary for action work; all other auxiliary systems not necessary for action are switched off.

'Action basic switching': Full readiness for the fuel systems, pipes, bunkers and the associated valves etc; the engine rooms divided into a number of units according to the number of shafts, as are the power plants; all power- or fuel-consuming installations to be fed directly; all lines and power-consuming installations not necessary for battle to be switched off in order to prevent additional damage in case of hits (there are exceptions as far as the powerplant is concerned); special attention to be paid to all those lines that cannot be observed directly from control positions or action stations.

Similar rules are applied to the other stations in other sections of the ship. The gunnery personnel had to be familiar with the ship's weapon systems and every sailor manned a particular position, be it gunner or ammunition handler. The gunnery personnel received additional instruction ashore. There were special courses run by naval training installations where they were trained as gun commander, gunlayer etc in order to assume these positions on board. In other sections the system was quite similar, the members of the ship's band, for example, receiving additional training as medical personnel, and even the administrative staff took part in the training for action stations.

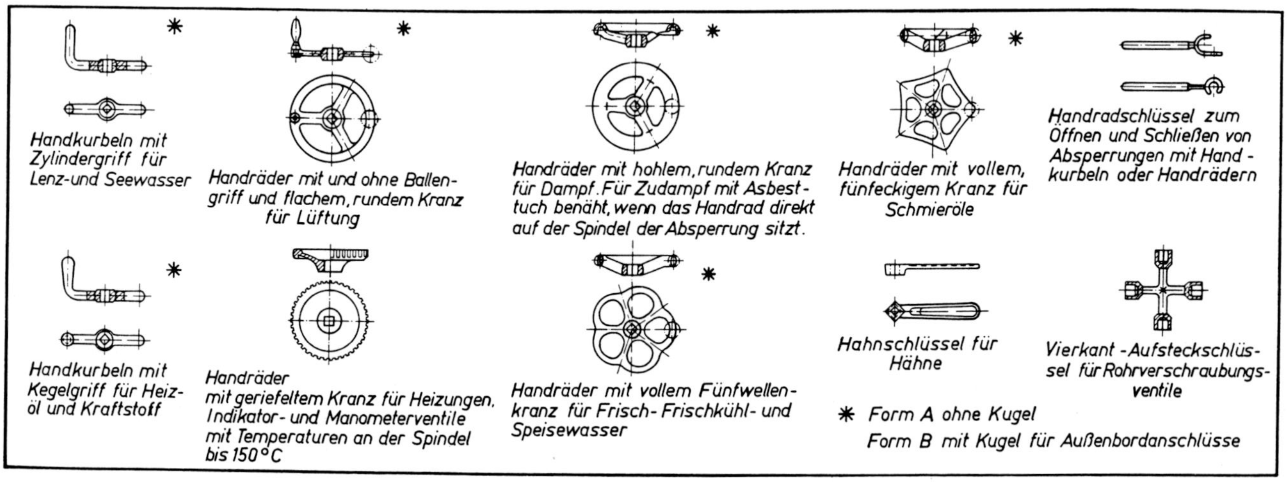

Another extract from German navy regulations, showing the different shapes of handwheels and other tools such as cranks and spanners.

Technical data of *Scharnhorst*

Displacement, official	26,000 tons
Displacement, real	
Standard 1935:	31,552 tons
Full load 1935:	37,822 tons
Standard 1943:	32,358 tons
Full load 1943:	38,703 tons
Maximum 1943:	39,643 tons
Design draught 1935:	8.69 m
Draught at 38.713 tons:	9.93 m
Armament:	9 x 28cm/L54.5 in three triple mountings 8 x 15cm/L55 in four twin mountings 4 x 15cm/L55 in single mountings 14 x 10.5cm/L65 AA guns in seven twin mountings 16 x 3.7cm/L83 AA guns in eight twin mountings 14 x 2cm/L65 in quadruple and single mountings
From 1942 on:	38 x 2cm/L65 in quadruple and single mountings 6 x 53.3cm torpedo tubes in two triple mountings
Aircraft:	3 x Aradao Ar 196
Machinery:	12 x Wagner high pressure superheated boilers 3 x sets geared turbines 3 x shafts 2 x rudders
Horsepower, design:	125,000
Horsepower, maximum:	160,050
Speed:	31 knots
Endurance:	7,100nm at 19 knots
Fuel capacity:	6,108 metric tons

Power plant:		
	6 x turbo generators	460kW each
	2 x turbo generators	230kW each
	2 x diesel generators	300kW each
	2 x diesel generators	150kW each

Complement 1943:	60 officers 1908 men

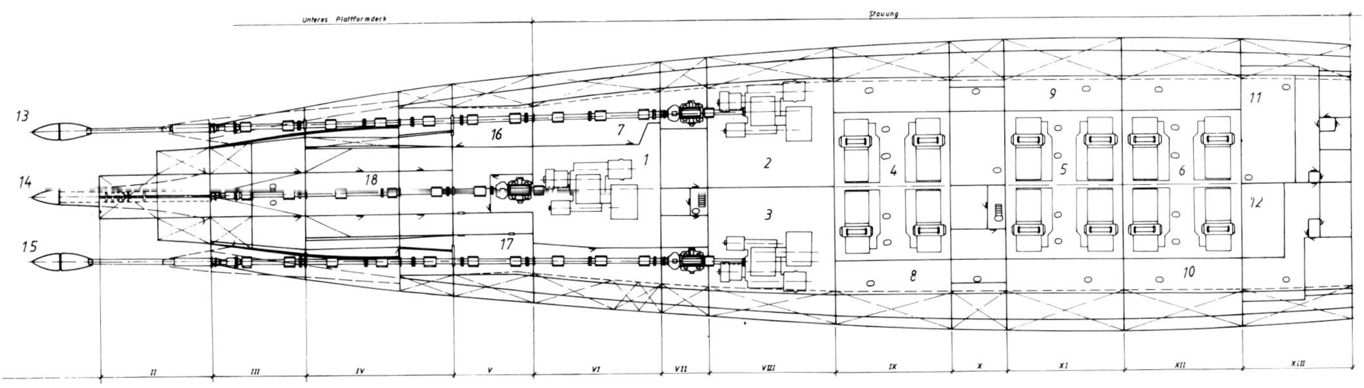

Machinery and armament in *Scharnhorst* and *Gneisenau*

1. turbine room, centre
2. turbine room, port
3. turbine room, starboard
4. boiler room 1
5. boiler room 2
6. boiler room 3
7. power plant 1
8. power plant 2
9. power plant 3
10. power plant 4
11. power plant 5
12. auxiliary boiler room
13. outer shaft, port
14. inner shaft
15. outer shaft, starboard
16. shaft tunnel, port
17. shaft tunnel, starboard
18. inner shaft tunnel

Armour

Belt	350mm KC, tapering to 170mm KC 150mm Wh, tapering to 70mm Wh (forecastle) 200mm Wh, tapering to 170mm Wh (rear part of the ship)
Transverse armour	150mm to 200mm KC bulkhead
Funnel base, bottom	20mm Wh
Citadel	45mm Wh 35mm Wh astern 20mm forward
Longitudinal splinter	20mm Wh bulkhead in thecitadel
Upper deck	50mm Wh
Armour deck	80–95mm Wh
Slopes of armour deck	105–110mm Wh
Torpedo bulkhead	45mm Ww
Fore conning tower	350mm KC (sides) 200mm KC (roof) 220mm KC (access tunnel) 350mm KC (front) 350mm KC (back)
Aft conning tower	100mm KC (sides) 50mm KC (roof) 100mm KC (access tunnel)
Hoods of the rangefinders on conning towers	100mm KC
Artillery director control tower, foretop	60mm KC 20mm KC (roof) 20mm KC (revolving hood)
AA-artillery director control tower	14mm KC
Barbettes of 28cm turrets	200mm KC (front, middle) 350mm KC (sides) 200mm KC (rear)
28cm turrets	360mm KC (front) 180mm KC (sides) 350mm KC (rear) 180mm KC (roof)
15cm turrets	140mm KC (front) 50mm KC (sides) 50mm KC (rear) 50mm KC (roof)
15cm single mountings	splinter protection shields 25mm
10.5cm	splinter protection shields 20mm

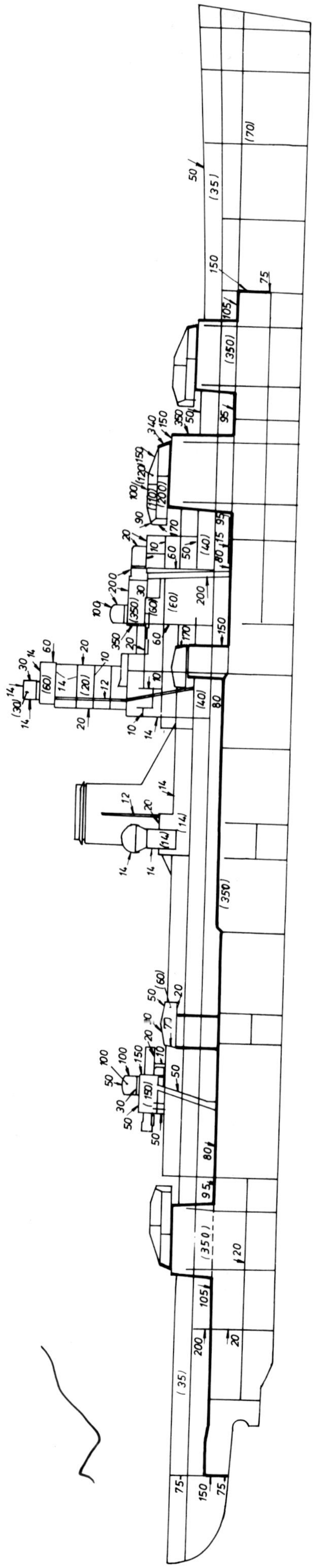

Gneisenau and *Scharnhorst* - a comparison of refits and reconstructions

Gneisenau

August 1938	Aircraft hangar reduced in size.
January 1939	Bows reconstructed, straight stem removed and replaced by Atlantic bow, funnel fitted with funnel cap.
May 1939	Old hawses sealed (2 port, 1 starboard) deck hawses fitted. Funnel cap slightly altered. Radio aerial mast on foretop removed and replaced by aerial mast on bridge tower. Hangar removed.
October 1939	Installation of a radar aerial FuMO on the revolving hood of the observation platform on the foretop.
January 1940	Admiral's bridge fitted with a roof. MES fitted.
February/ March 1940	Catapult on turret C and crane removed.
January 1941	2cm AA gun in quadruple mounting fitted on a revolving platform. Hoods from rangefinder on turret A removed. Single 2cm AA guns C30 replaced by similar guns of the C38 type. Radar set FuMO replaced.
Brest 1941/1942	Radar set FuMO installed astern. Quadruple 2cm AA gun removed, three 2cm AA guns C38 in quadruple mountings fitted instead on turret B, the funnel platform and on top of the new hangar. New hangar fitted with side-mounted doors and internally mounted catapult. Torpedo tubes fitted. The planned tripod mainmast (similar to that on *Scharnhorst*) was never fitted.

Scharnhorst

June 1939	Straight stem removed and replaced by Atlantic bow, ship's hull extended. Aircraft hangar enlarged, catapult fitted to hangar roof. Mainmast behind the funnel removed, new tripod mainmast fitted some 27m aft. Funnel fitted with funnel cap.
December 1939	Radar set FuMO 22 mounted on foretop.
1940	MES-installation fitted with the cable loop fitted above the armour belt. Catapult on 28cm turret C and associated crane removed.
1941	Wings of the bridge reduced to half their original length. Torpedo tubes in two triple mountings mounted on main deck on the sides of the hangar. These torpedo tubes came from the light cruiser *Nuernberg*.
1942	Radar set FuMO 22 on foretop replaced by FuMO 27. Additional second FuMO 27 fitted on the aft conning tower. Admiral's bridge fitted with a roof. Platform base around funnel enlarged to mount a quadruple 2cm AA gun. Platforms fitted on both sides of the catapult base to mount two quadruple 2cm AA guns. Rangefinder on 28cm turret A removed and openings sealed. Both 15cm turrets Bb I and Stb I (port and starboard) fitted with a platform to take additional quadruple 2cm AA guns on army mountings, ready for the Channel Dash. 28cm turret B also fitted with additional quadruple 2cm AA gun (for the Channel Dash, too).

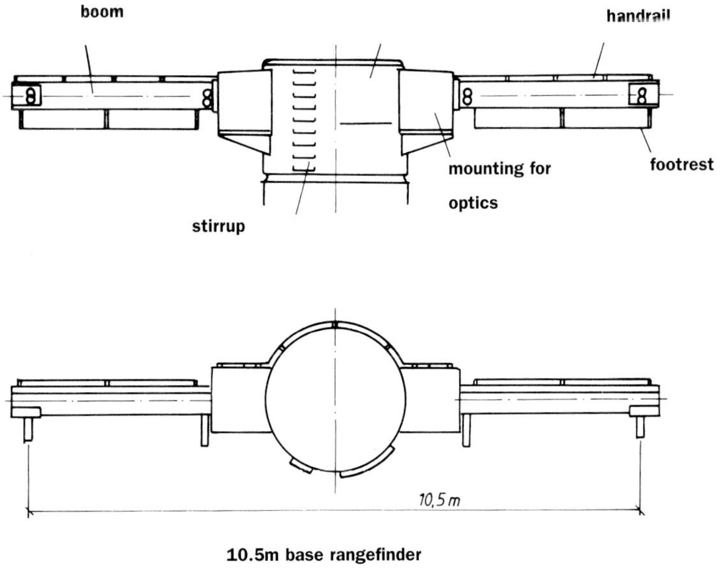

10.5m base rangefinder

Mounted – foretop
– aft conning tower
also in similar configuration: 28cm turrets A (later removed), B and C

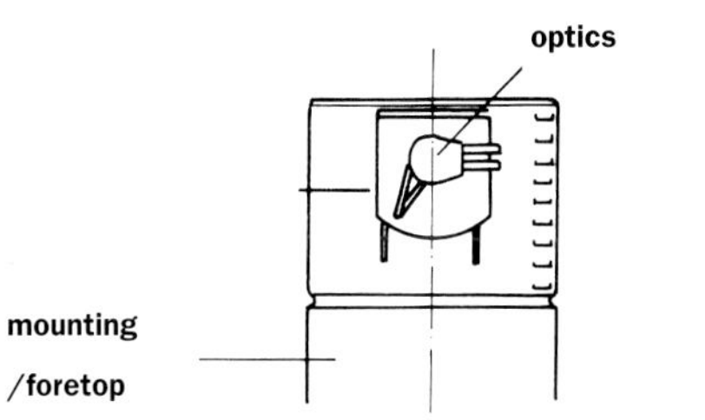

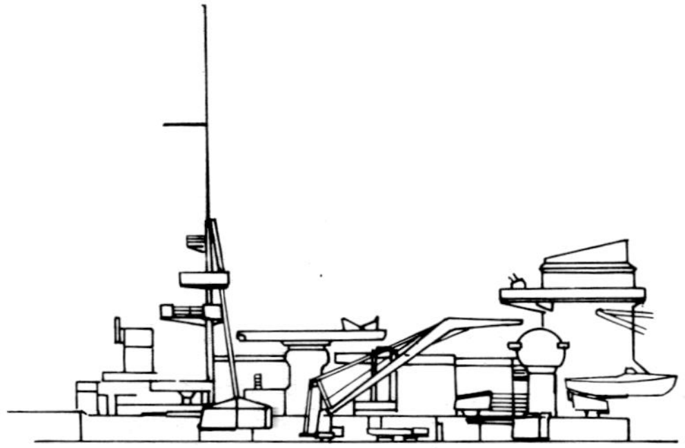

Scharnhorst before reconstruction

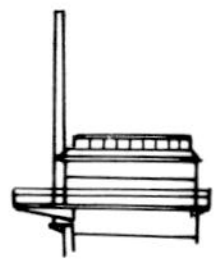

Funnel of *Scharnhorst* and *Gneisenau* before reconstruction

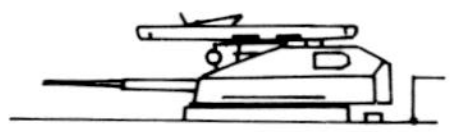

Catapult removed during reconstruction

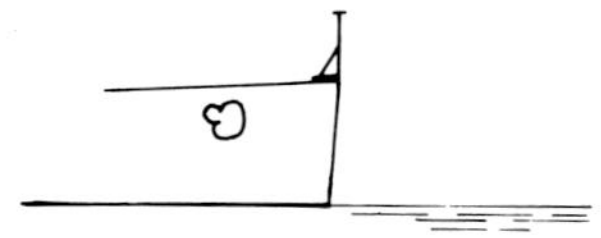

Bow of *Scharnhorst* and *Gneisenau* before reconstruction

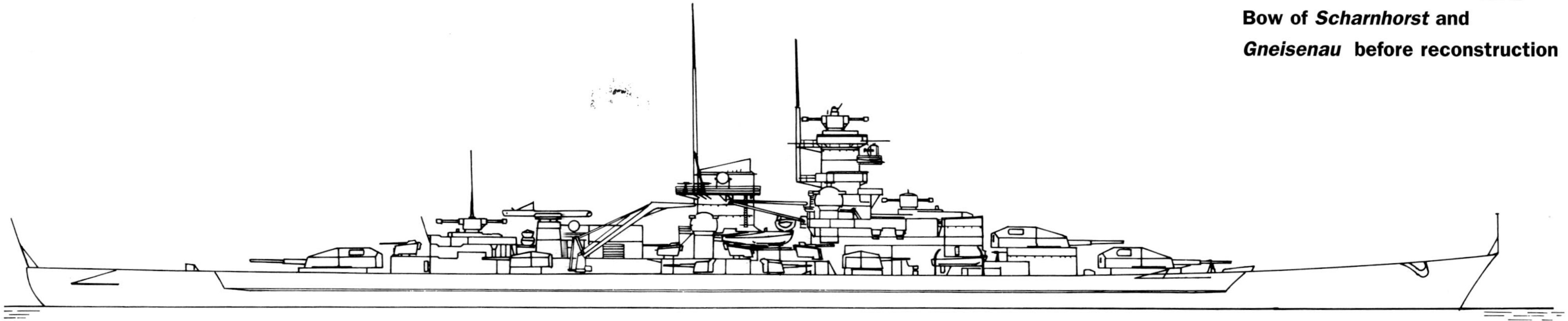

Gneisenau after reconstruction, 1940

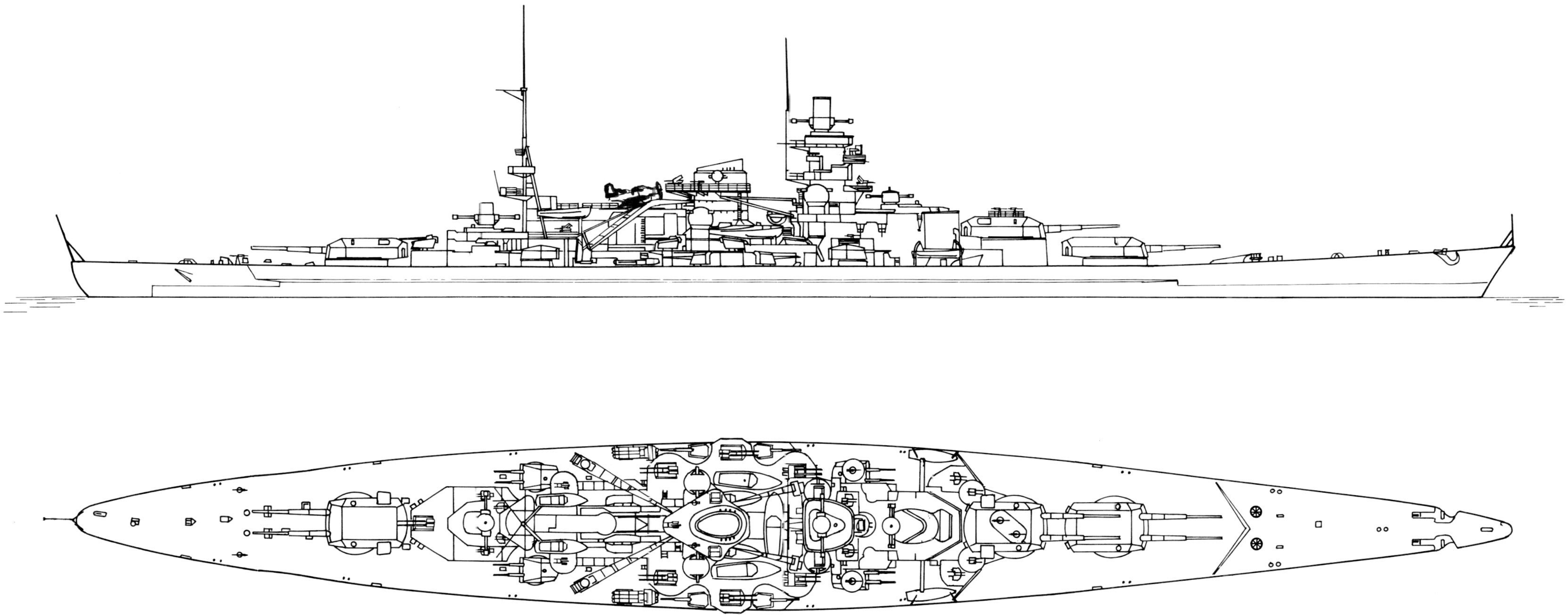

Planned reconstruction of *Gneisenau*, 1942

28cm gun L/54.5 Sk34 with trainable turret C34 in triple mounting:

side view

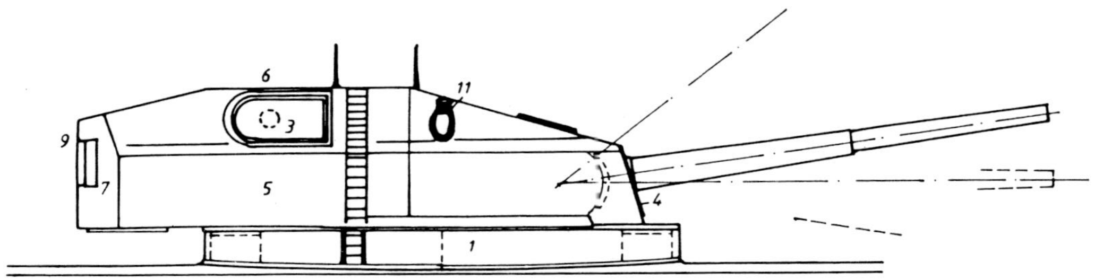

top view

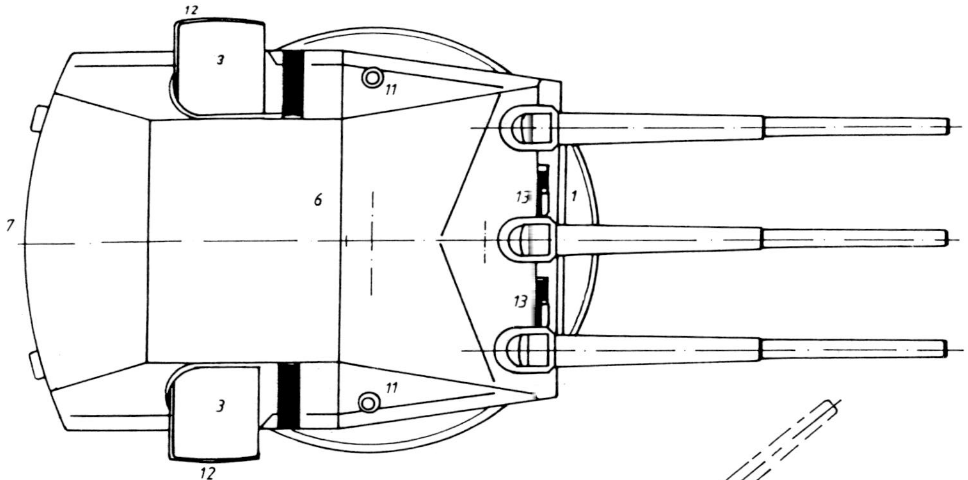

front view

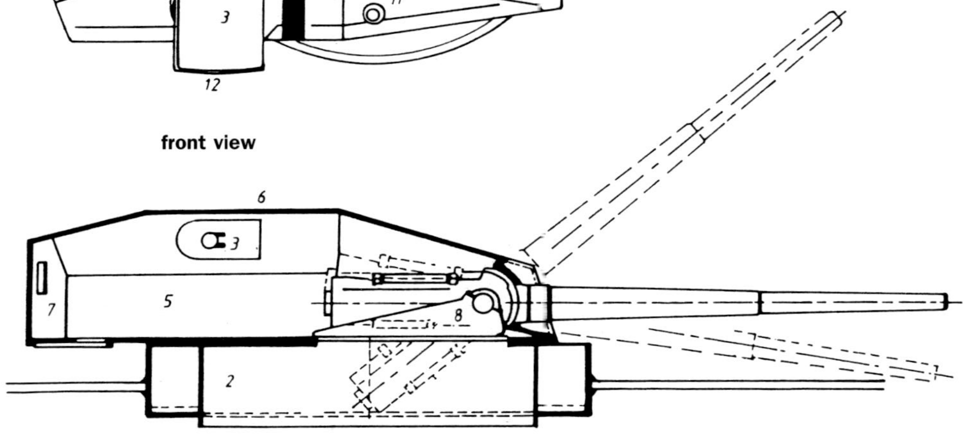

front view

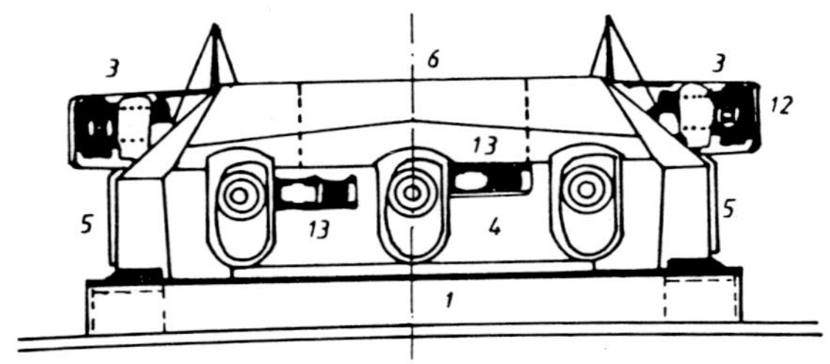

sectional view

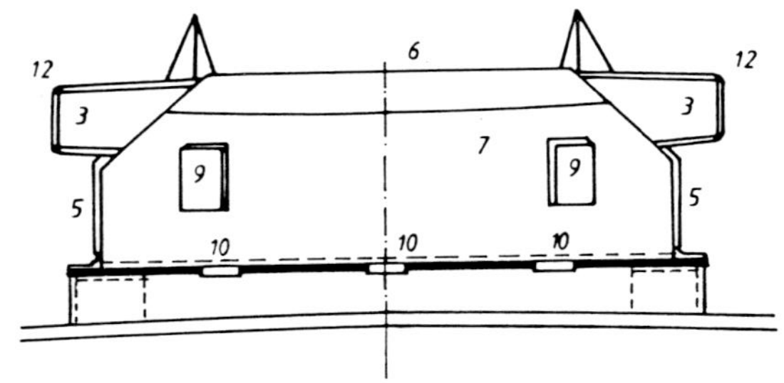

1 barbette
2 training cylinder
3 10.5m base rangefinder
4 turret front
5 turret side walls
6 turret roof
7 rear side
8 trunnion bracket
9 case ejection port
10 vents
11 turret periscope
12 armour hoods for rangefinder
13 armour front

Scharnhorst career notes

Launched 3 October 1936, commissioned 7 January 1939. After the completion of trials in the Summer of 1939, refits in the *Kriegsmarinewerft* 'naval shipyard' at Wilhelmshaven.

After the beginning of the Second World War there were several joint operations with her sistership *Gneisenau* in September and October 1939. The first operation was unsuccessful, but the second one led to the sinking of the British armed merchant-cruiser *Rawalpindi*. Another operation in February 1940 was again unsuccessful. Early in April 1940 she took part in the operation against Norway, where she fought a running battle with the British battle-cruiser *Renown*.

The next operation in June 1940 led her to the north, where, among others, she sank the British carrier *Glorious*. During this battle *Scharnhorst* suffered a hit from a torpedo and at the end of June had to return home for repairs. In February 1941 – once again together with *Gneisenau* – she made another dash to the North Atlantic for commercial raiding operations.

In March 1941 she entered the harbour of Brest. As the threat from air attacks became more and more imminent she returned home in February 1942, accompanied by *Gneisenau* and the heavy cruiser *Prinz Eugen*. After extensive repairs and refits and several aborted attempts to leave home waters she managed to reach Norway in March 1943. In September 1943 she left Norway for an operation against Spitzbergen, this time together with *Tirpitz*. After *Tirpitz* was put out of action, *Scharnhorst* remained the only battleworthy capital ship of the Kriegsmarine in Norway.

In the month of December 1943, during an attempt to intercept an allied convoy, *Scharnhorst* was sunk by superior British forces.

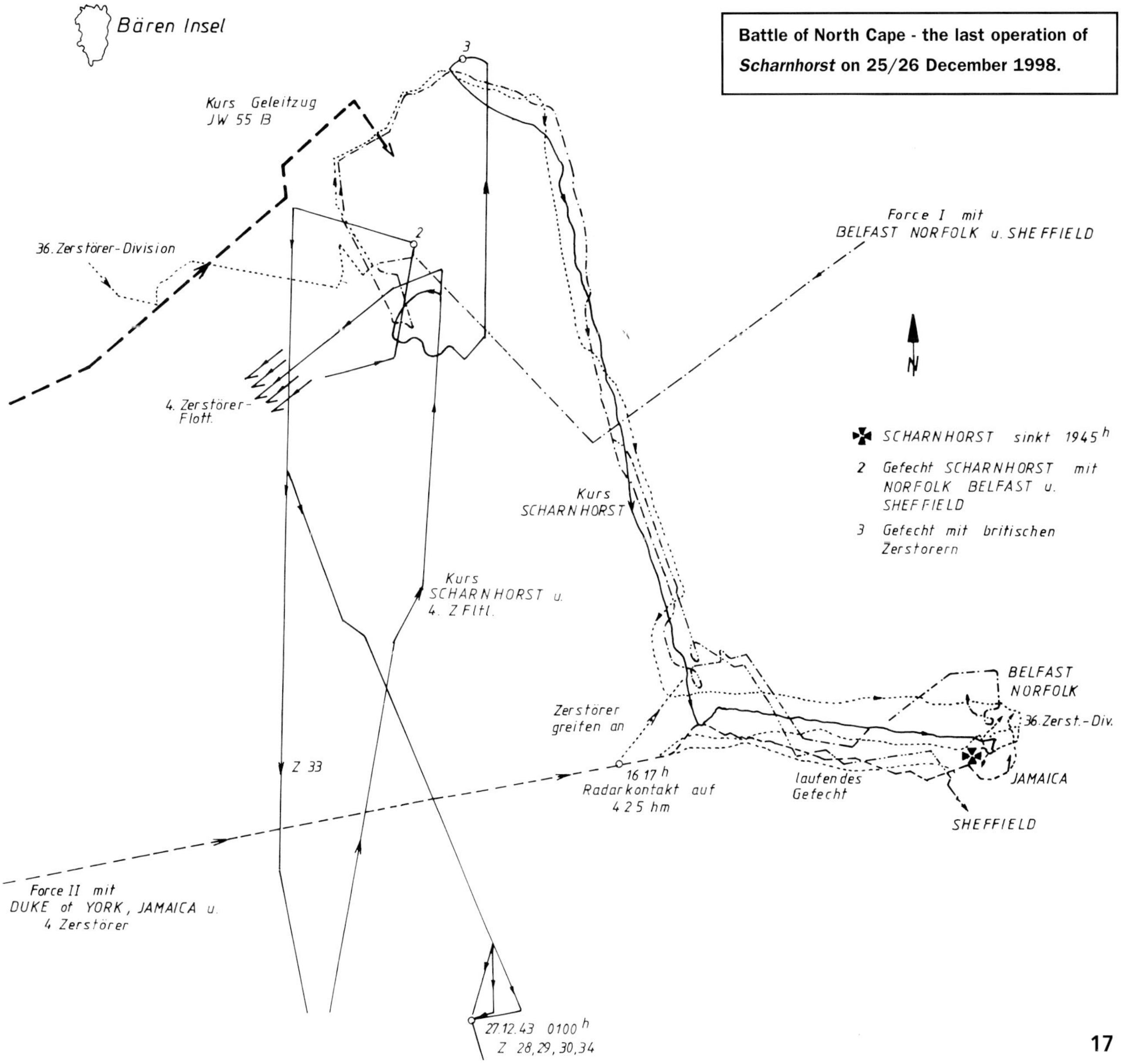

Battle of North Cape - the last operation of *Scharnhorst* on 25/26 December 1998.

A pictorial history of *Scharnhorst* (*Gneisenau*)

Scharnhorst a few days before her launch.
This photograph affords a good view of the mighty hull resting on the launching slip of the *Kriegsmarinewerft* 'navy yard' at Wilhelmshaven. Note the break shields and the stop anchor hanging down.

3 October 1936; the ship has been named. Slowly first, then faster and faster the giant hull slips into the narrow basin of building yard of the *Kriegsmarinewerft*. It is remarkable to see how this difficult task was solved. As usual in Wilhelmshaven, a large crowd gathered to watch the launch.

Starboard view of *Gneisenau* as she leaves Kiel harbour, 1938.

Compare the above photograph with this starboard view of *Scharnhorst*, taken on 13 April 1939.

Another view of the midship section of *Gneisenau*, July 1938. Both catapults carry an aircraft as this was the period of intensive trials with different types of aircraft. The wings of the aircraft in front are still folded up.

***Scharnhorst* in 1939, seen here in the Forth of Kiel, made fast to buoy No 12. She has not yet been refitted; her bow anchors can be seen in their hawses, two on port and one on starboard, and both booms have been erected. The jack flag has been retouched by a censor.**

Starboard quarter view of *Scharnhorst* in Kiel. Two masthead flags are hoisted, one on the bridge tower and one on the mainmast, both being the *Reichskriegsflagge* 'war ensign'. The ship's company parading on the quarterdeck indicates a special occasion. A group of officers and seamen are waiting near the gangway, in anticipation of a high-ranking visitor who is most probably on board the boat, the bow of which is visible on this photo, approaching the ship. Note the aircraft with folded-up wings resting on the catapult on top of turret C.

Scharnhorst in the Firth of Kiel after her refit. She is now equipped with an Atlantic bow and a funnel cap; the mainmast was moved further aft, and the hangar was modified. On the front catapult, an Arado Ar 196 can already be seen.

Gneisenau after her major refit, captured on film on 13 April 1939. The most significant features of this refit were the new bow, the funnel cap and the modified aircraft hangar.

Mainmast of *Scharnhorst*. It is impossible to decipher the flag signals flying from the yards. The flags were coloured, each flag having a particular meaning either as a letter, a group of letters, a number, or a message.

In the winter of 1939/1940, the activities of the *Kriegsmarine* were seriously hampered. With increasing thickness of the ice in the Baltic, operations became more and more difficult. Finally most ships were transferred to the North Sea, where they were also hampered by ice but less critically. This photograph, taken in January or February 1940, shows the midship section of *Gneisenau* in Kiel. The layer of ice on the waters of the Firth of Kiel was so thick that it could be covered with planks, and one could walk to and from the ships instead of having to use a boat.

Finally, the ships were transferred to the North Sea. This photograph was taken in February 1940 in the mouth of the Jade, the approach to Wilhelmshaven. A starboard view from the bridge of *Scharnhorst* shows one of the escorting destroyers following the battleship through the drifting ice, a difficult task. Behind the destroyer, *Gneisenau* is visible.

Gneisenau in drifting ice passing Schilling-Reede on the Jade. On the quarter deck, the ship's company is on parade. In order to provide space for so many men, the barrels of 28cm turret C were elevated. One of the ship's aircraft can be seen on the catapult.

Operation Juno, raid of the two battleships *Gneisenau* and *Scharnhorst*, together with the heavy cruiser *Admiral Hipper* and some destroyers, into the northern North Sea up to Arctic waters. In the course of this operation, the British aircraft carrier *Glorious* was sunk. Taken with a telephoto lens from *Scharnhorst*, following in the wake of *Gneisenau*, this photograph provides an overwhelming impression of the action against *Glorious* and her escort destroyers. Turrets A and B of *Gneisenau* have just fired a salvo.

Operation Cerberus in February 1942, the Channel Dash of the German major surface warships *Scharnhorst*, *Gneisenau* and *Prinz Eugen* to enter home waters. This photograph of *Scharnhorst* depicts the two 28cm turrets A and B. They are in their basic positions, the barrel ports are protected from spray by canvas bags. Her AA armament is fully operational. The barrels of the 10.5cm, 3.7cm and 2cm guns are elevated and all guns manned. The 2cm quadruple mounting on top of turret C is well visible, as are the two 15cm turrets Stb I (starboard I) and Bb I (port I). Turret Stb I has been trained sidewards. All rangefinders and the radar aerials attached to the revolving hoods are turned towards the enemy. Note the rectangular device positioned above the two AA control platforms, it is probably a radar aerial, too. All platforms hold observers.

A forward view from the quarterdeck, this photograph of *Scharnhorst* was taken in the Baltic in 1942. On the left, partially covered by the 15cm guns trained to port, the light cruiser *Nuernberg* can be seen.

Scharnhorst in Norwegian waters in 1943. Highly visible are the struts of the tripod main mast and also the aerial of the FuMO-radar on the aft artillery control tower. The ship's band is playing, the occasion presumably being a colours ceremony. These were held on special occasions such as *Skageraktag* 'Battle of Jutland Day'.

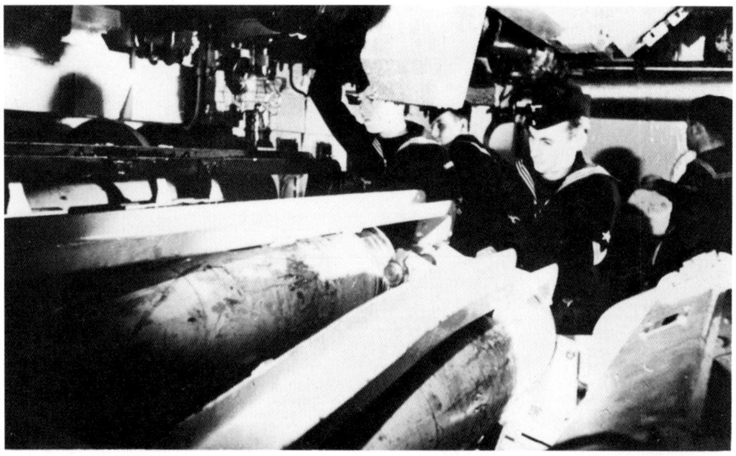

Views taken from inside the transmitting station for 28cm ammunition on *Gneisenau*.

Another photograph of the transmitting station for 28cm ammunition. The powder cartridges can be seen on the conveyor band.

The interior of a 28cm turret, with a powder cartridge ready for loading.

View taken from inside one of the boiler rooms.

Part of the permanent maintenance and service duties for the ships armament was cleaning the guns. Here, members of the crew of *Gneisenau* are seen washing the 28cm barrels of turret C. As the base of the catapult can still be seen on top of the turret it suggests that this is an early photograph.

Operation Berlin, a commerce raiding sortie of the two battleships *Gneisenau* and *Scharnhorst* in the Atlantic, spring 1941. This photograph shows the midship section of *Gneisenau*. Many details are visible, such as the 10.5cm guns of the AA armament, the directors for the AA armament and the platforms of the bridge tower. The white uniforms of the crew indicate that the climate in these latitudes is better than at home.

Operation Berlin; *Gneisenau* is seen here during one of the many refuellings. This photograph clearly shows that the ships of this class were poor sea boats. Due to their low freeboard, the decks were usually awash.

This photograph of *Gneisenau* was also taken during an operation in the Atlantic. Note how active the censor has been: the equipment of the foretop, including the rangefinder, has been retouched.

This photograph of *Gneisenau* was taken from the submarine U 124, which in March 1941 was provided with fuel and other supplies. The ship's company is watching the operation.

Training the ship's crew in the Baltic, with seamen doing boat drill. Seen here is the hoisting up of a cutter, which, on small vessels, is usually a manoeuvre with all hands. The cutter attached to the davits is being hoisted up by an endless chain of men until it can be secured to the davits. The sailors virtually run in a circle and always return to the front in order to give a helping hand. The whole manoeuvre is accompanied by the rhythm of the whistles of the boatswain's mates. In German naval slang, this is called a *Kutterlaeufer* 'cutter run'.

Scharnhorst during Operation Berlin in the Atlantic. When operating in remote areas, opportunities such as these were used to offer the crew some entertainment. Here they have assembled on the quarterdeck to listen to the ship's band playing, although safety measures were still maintained with all action stations manned throughout.

View of *Gneisenau*, taken from the bow. The white caps of the crew indicate that the photograph must have been taken before Autumn 1939, as white caps were worn in the summer only. The two 28cm turrets A and B have been rotated to port or to their port end position respectively.

Embarkation of ammunition on *Scharnhorst*. Safety, of course, was the prime necessity when handling ammunition. The powder cartridges were delivered in special containers and the use of a trolley may give an idea of how heavy these containers were. In the magazines and shell rooms the ammunition was stored in racks which protected them from shock and jolt and also from the influences of rough seas.

Brest 1941/1942. It is fairly difficult to see that this photograph depicts *Scharnhorst* in dry dock. To the right of the crane, parts of the bridge tower, the funnel and the mainmast are visible.

Training in peacetime on the twin-barrelled 3.7cm AA guns. Note the numerous members of the gun crew and also the handheld rangefinders operated by several sailors in the background above the gun's barrels.

Training in wartime. Here the gun crews of two of the twin-barrelled 10.5cm AA guns and one of the single 15cm guns are seen during their combat training.

Scharnhorst in heavy seas. This photograph was taken astern from amidships starboard. The turrets of the secondary artillery have been trained to the starboard side.

Midship of *Scharnhorst*, starboard side. Note the struts of the tripod mainmast and the opened hatch of the rangefinder on the 28cm turret C. Above the turret, the rangefinder on the after control platform can be seen.

Training on the quadruple 2cm AA gun on *Scharnhorst*. There were not many opportunities for such training during the ships lay days in Brest and La Pallice as there were numerous British air attacks. The members of the gun crew all belong to the 3rd starboard watch (indicated by three tapes on the right sleeve). The gun is one of the 2cm quadruple mountings fitted to the fore 15cm twin turrets (port and starboard).

Aerial view of one of the 2cm quadruple mountings on the sides of the hangar. Below the gun one of the triple mounting torpedo tubes can be seen which were fitted in France, but never used. The loading drill on *Scharnhorst* is shown here.

View of the 20cm turret C on *Gneisenau*, taken in peacetime. On the catapult attached to the turret the final version of the ship's aircraft can be seen, the Arado Ar 196. Note the long cylinder mounted underneath the catapult, which is a compressed-air cylinder. Highly compressed air was used to propel the catapult when launching an aircraft.

Aircraft being catapulted to starboard. The AA armament is fully manned, the barrel being elevated towards the sky. In the foreground there is a close-range 2cm gun in quadruple mounting, behind it three of the twin-barrelled 10.5cm AA guns. Also visible is one of the 15cm guns in single mounting. It is interesting to note that there is a blast bag fitted to the barrel. This photograph was presumably taken in the Baltic in 1942.

View taken from above into the opened hangar. Members of the crew are servicing the three aircraft belonging to the ship; one of them is being prepared for take-off.

A view inside the ship's conning tower. The ship's executive officer is in charge with assitance from the damage control officer and other personnel such as runners and couriers.

A view inside the ship's engine control position, which is the battle station of the chief engineer officer. He, too, is assisted by personnel for the transmission of messages.

One of the boiler rooms of *Scharnhorst* where one of the Saacke-burners is being removed.

A view inside one of the three shaft tunnels. Two members of the watch remove a lubrication oil sample from one of the many bearings.

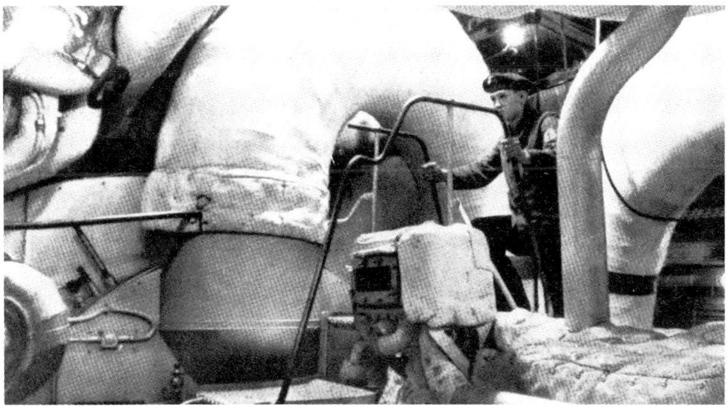

The steam propelling the turbines came through pipes into the appropriate turbine rooms, where it was directed to the jets. Under normal battle conditions, two boiler rooms supplied one set of turbines and all three installations operated separately from each other. Of course, all boilers could supply their own sets of turbines only, but under battle conditions all boilers had to supply all turbines. They were all connected to each other and could then supply as much steam as necessary. There were additional pipe connections which enabled, for example, the port boilers to supply the starboard turbines with steam. In such cases, the appropriate pipe connections were switched. The steam pipes carried a thick coat of insulation cladding in order to prevent the rooms from being overheated, but also to prevent large heat loss. They were not straight, but were equipped with many bends and also, most important of all, the *Dampfboegen* 'steam pipe elbows'. These had the task of absorbing and compensating tensions in the pipes which were the result of the many speed changes effected in rapid sequence on a warship.

View of one of the central power control rooms of *Scharnhorst*.

One of the diesel-powered dynamo rooms of *Scharnhorst* with two diesel engines visible. Switchboards are visible in the background.

Scharnhorst in dry dock, taken from astern. Compare the size of the dock workers with the size of the propellers and the two rudders which are fitted in a slightly inclined position. They were positioned outside the waterflow of the propellers.

Camouflage patterns

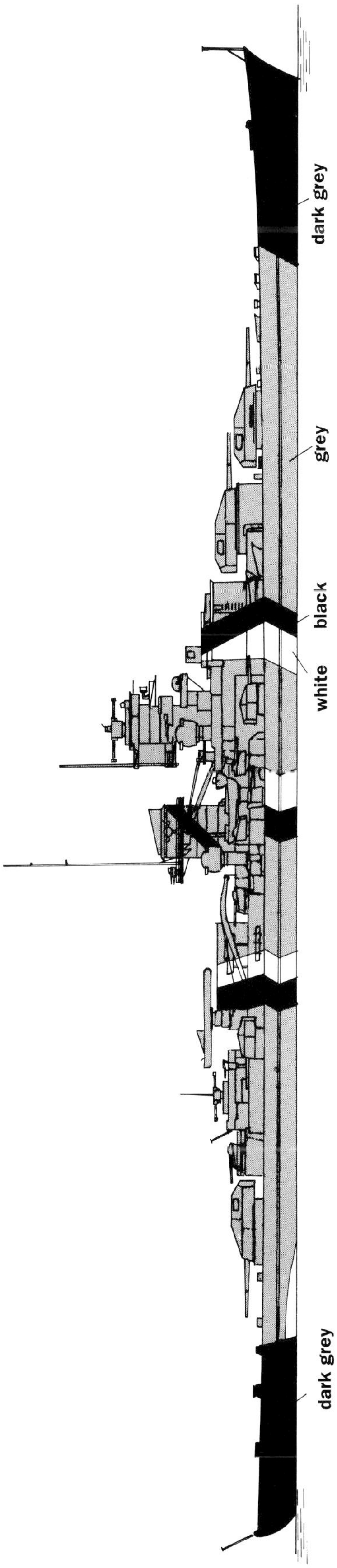

Gneisenau
Autumn 1940 (port and starboard sides carried similar patterns)

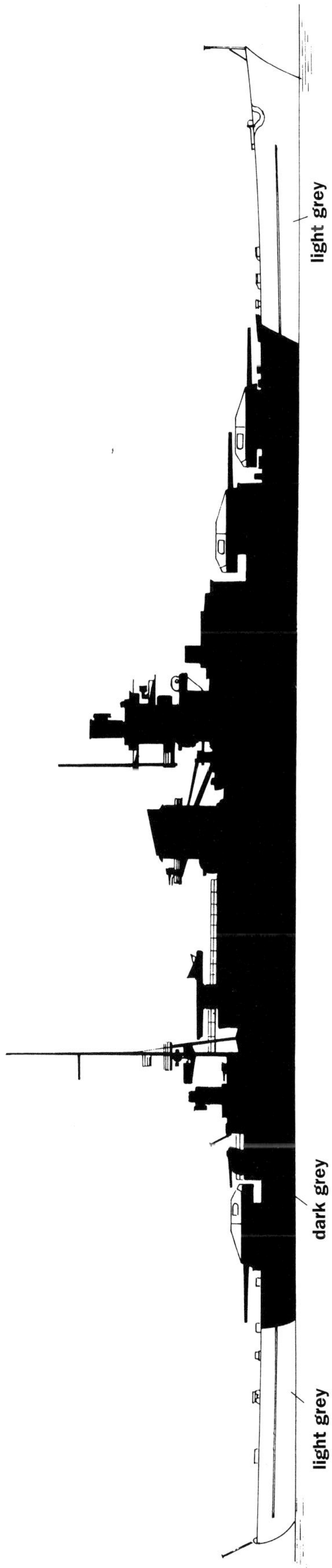

Scharnhorst
Norway (port and starboard sides carried similar patterns)
disrupted pattern

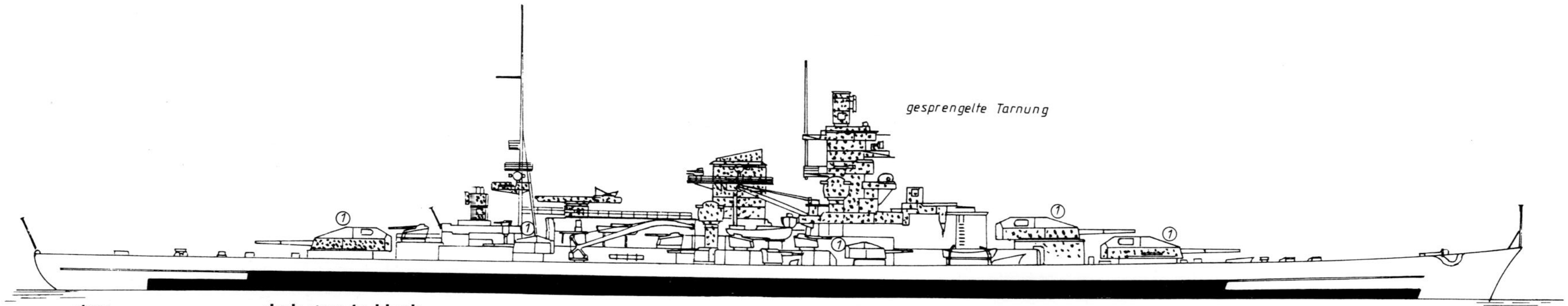

Scharnhorst
Channel Dash February 1942
(port and starboard sides carried similar patterns)

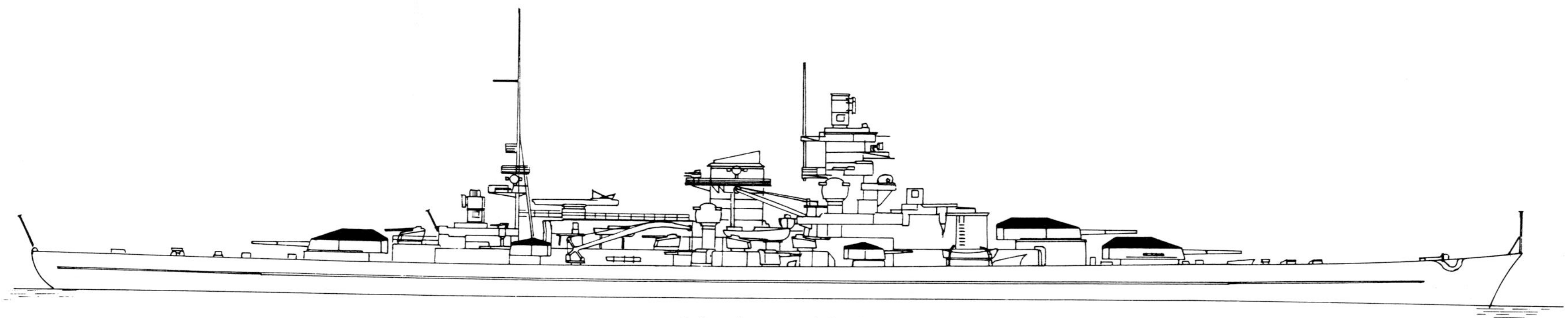

Scharnhorst and *Gneisenau*
January 1941 in the Atlantic
Turret roofs of main and secondary armament painted yellow

Scharnhorst as scale model

Two shipyard models of *Scharnhorst*, affording good views of both the port and starboard sides. Both models show the ship with her typical features after refit: Atlantic bow, funnel cap, modified aircraft hangar, and, at the end of the hangar, the large tripod mainmast. While the upper model is already equipped with the radar aerial on top of the bridge tower, this aerial is still missing on the lower model. The top model also carries the catapult on the roof of 28cm turret C, which the lower model does not. On the lower model, however, the aircraft crane behind the aft turret is still visible, which was removed together with the catapult. Both models are still shown with the rangefinder attached to turret A.

A model of *Scharnhorst*, built by Mr W Fraider for the Kuestenmuseum in Wilhelmshaven, scale 1:100. It is seen here in the old rooms of the museum.

The model today, an overall view of the starboard side.
The photographs on the wall depict the *Kaiserlichewerft* at Wilhelmshaven in 1918 and some installations of the naval arsenal. To the left of these photographs, there are additional images of ships of the imperial navy, the Weimar era and the *Kriegsmarine.* In front of *Scharnhorst* there are models of the light cruiser *Emden* and several destroyers, all built to the same scale.

Rear part of *Scharnhorst*, affording a good view of the starboard and midship propellers, their shafts, the shaft bosses and the rudders. On the quarterdeck, hatches and stern capstans are visible. Also visible are the folded-up propeller protector, the plate with the ship's name and the upper edge of the armour belt. Note the continuous line of scuttles on the hull. In front of 28cm turret C is the aft superstructure with the aft 10.5cm AA gun in twin mounting, and behind and above it tho aft bridge with the director for the 10.5cm gun and a radar aerial attached to the revolving hood of the director. Note the two single 2cm guns near the railing.

Amidships view from the 28cm turret C to the bridge tower. At the lower section of the hull, the starboard bilge keel is visible, as well as the top edge of the armour belt. Also visible are the aft 15cm turret and the aircraft crane. Behind the crane are the torpedo tubes in triple mounting which were fitted in Brest and two 15cm guns in single mountings. Above the 15cm guns in single mountings the starboard 10.5cm guns in twin mountings can be seen, along with the long aircraft hangar. On top of the hangar roof is the catapult on its revolving mount, and there is one of the three aircraft of the type Aradao Ar 196 on the catapult. On the side of the hangar, a 2cm AA gun in quadruple mounting has been added. Behind the hangar is the tripod mainmast with its platforms, the lower one of these carries a searchlight. In front of the hangar is the funnel with a further 2cm AA gun in quadruple mounting fitted to its rear. On the rear side of the bridge tower are additional small cranes which were used for hoisting the ship's boats. Also visible on the side of the funnel is one of the AA directors, called *Wackeltopf* 'shaky pot' in German naval slang.

Another sectional view of the midship with the mainmast. Note the many Marx-floats stored on the side of the aircraft hangar. On photographs of the original ship these floats can seldom be seen. Such a float consisted of a square frame, the floating body of which was made of metal or other materials. It was hollow and filled with a water-resistant and floatable material, the inner part fitted with grating. Marx-floats served as additional means of rescue. Under normal conditions they were quite useful but during a battle there was a danger of them being damaged or destroyed by direct hits or splinters, rendering them useless.

Midship section of *Scharnhorst*. Once again, because of the position of the model, only the starboard side can be seen. This photograph affords a good view of the bridge tower with its platforms and also the front part of the bridge. On the right are the 28cm turrets A and B, and between the barbette and the bridge there is a 2cm AA gun in a single mounting. In front of the fore 15cm guns in twin mountings there is a boat attached to its davits. On the turret roof of this gun is a 2cm AA gun in a quadruple mounting, which was fitted in Brest. The folded-down wing of the bridge can be seen above the boat, and on the side of the front mast there is the fore AA-director. On top of the bridge is the fore conning tower with its 6m base rangefinder. The platforms are equipped with searchlights and light AA-weapons as well as all sorts of additional optical aiming devices. Between the funnel and bridge tower is a large motor boat. Attached to the rear side of the bridge tower is a mast which is also referred to as the foremast. On top of the bridge tower is the main artillery director control tower, consisting of the director control tower itself and the 10.5m base rangefinder with its revolvable hood. Later, a radar platform and aerial was fitted to the director control platform and in Brest another open observation platform was fitted to this radar platform.

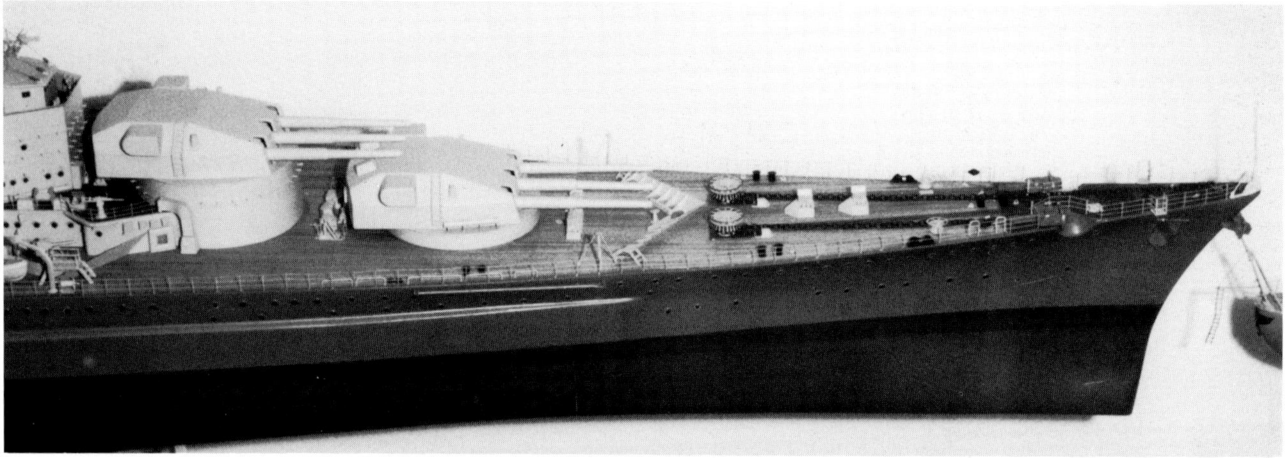

The forecastle with a view of the bow with the front anchor and the swinging boom. The two side anchors lie in their hawses on deck, held by the chain cables coming from the chain lockers and the capstans. In front of 28cm turret A is the breakwater, and there are a large number of scuttles on the ship's side. This model is meant to show *Scharnhorst* at the time of her leaving Brest but there is one mistake: by this time, 28cm turret A was no longer fitted with a rangefinder and the openings had been sealed with armour plates.

More detailed photographs of the funnel group. The two views of port and starboard are almost identical, apart from minor details. Note the motor boat between funnel and bridge tower and the 'Otter' devices of the fore mine clearing gear stored near the funnel.

This photograph affords a detailed view of the bridge tower with the 3.7cm AA gun in twin mounting in front of the AA-director control tower SL6. Also visible is the 2cm AA gun in quadruple mounting on top of the fore 15cm turret.

Seen here are the observation platform additionally fitted in Brest, the radar aerial FuMO and a 2cm AA gun in a single mounting on the director control platform.

A view of the bridge with the fore conning tower and the bridge tower, which carries a special platform with an additional small radar set. Note the many openings on the roof of the conning tower which could be equipped with periscopes and optical aiming devices. The box-shaped closed platform on the bridge tower is the admiral's bridge. The platform below this carries a 3.7cm AA gun and several aiming devices. Between the conning tower and 28cm turret B, a 2cm AA gun in single mounting and a 3.7cm AA gun in twin mounting can be seen.

A photograph of the starboard side of the same model.

The two 28cm turrets A and B. The two long tube-like containers attached to the side of turret A and the conning tower are containers for spare parts, tools and devices necessary for aiming the large guns.

The plans

Plan 01 Internal profile and deck plan according to official set of drawings (before reconstruction)

Plan 02 Upper deck, superstructure and bridges according to general plan (before reconstruction)

Plan 03 Main deck and middle deck according to official set of drawings

Plan 04 Lower deck and upper platform deck according to official set of drawings

Plan 05 Middle platform deck, lower platform deck and hold according to official set of drawings

Plan 06 Transverse sections I-XIV according to official set of drawings

Plan 07 Transverse sections XIV-XXI according to official set of drawings

Plan 08 Main frame

Plan 09 Body and profile plan

Plan 10 General arrangements with internal profile and deck plan (after reconstructions)

Plan 11 Aerial arrangement plan according to general plan (after reconstructions)

Plan 12 Sectional drawings according to general plan (after reconstruction) and rig (August 1942)

Plan 13 General plan: upper deck, superstructure and bridges

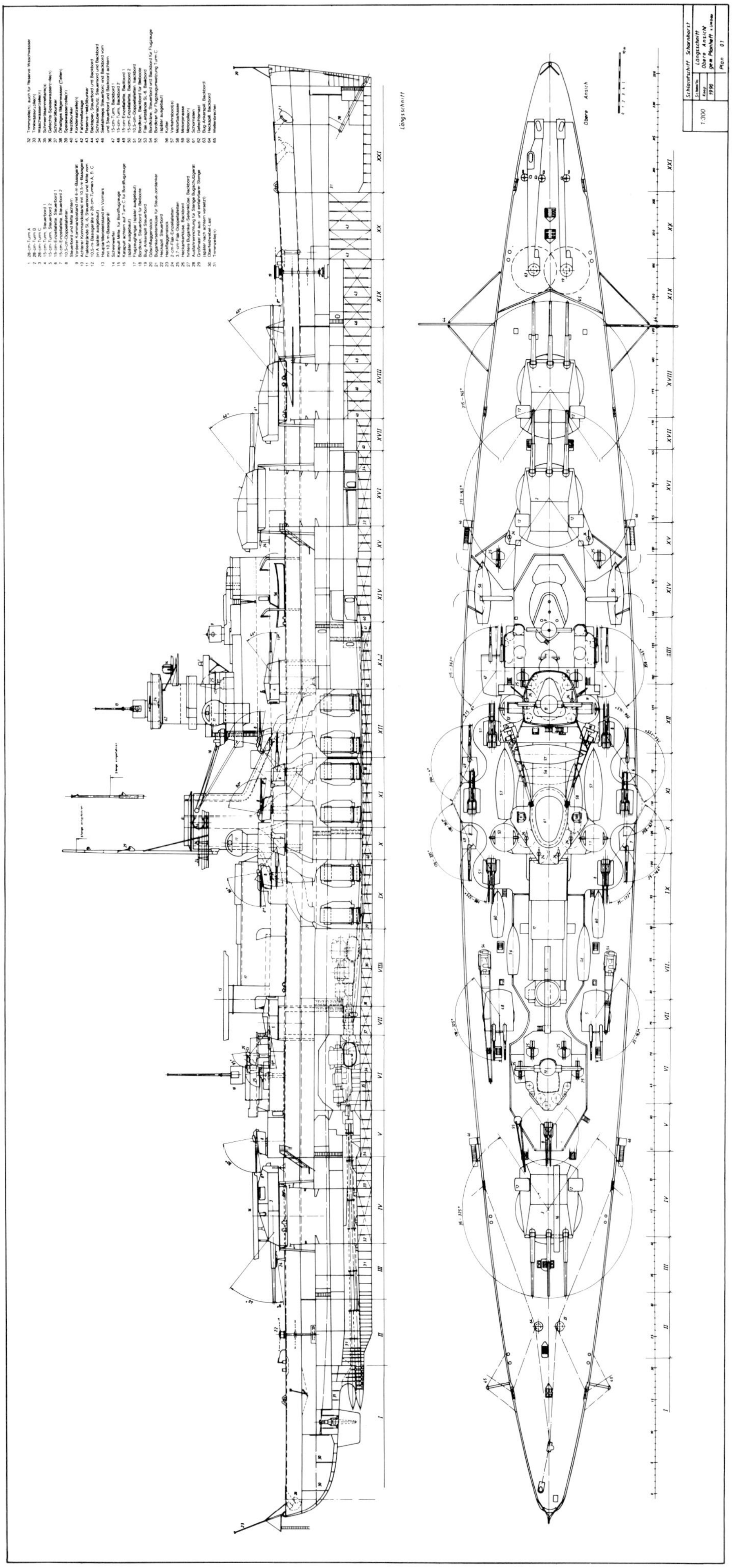

Plan 01

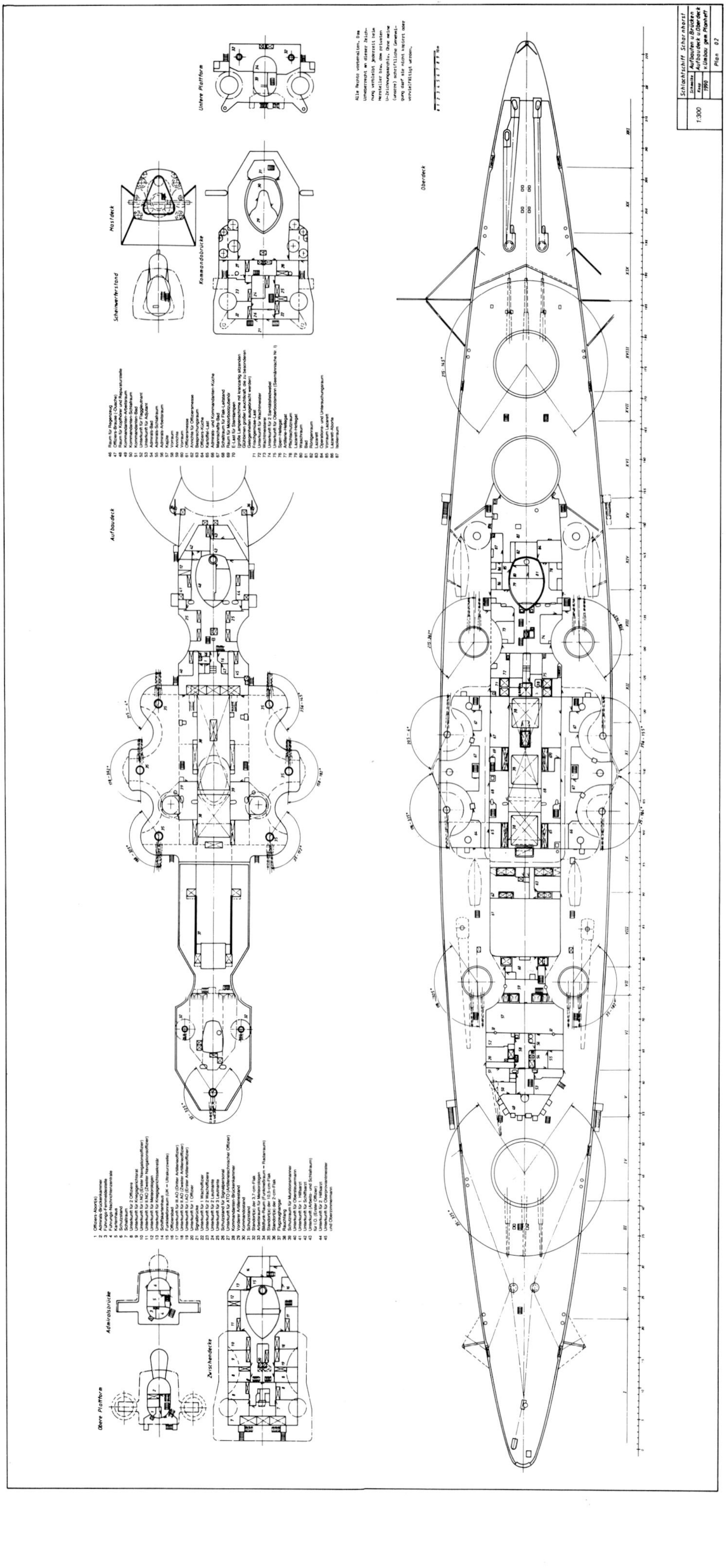

Plan 02

Plan 03

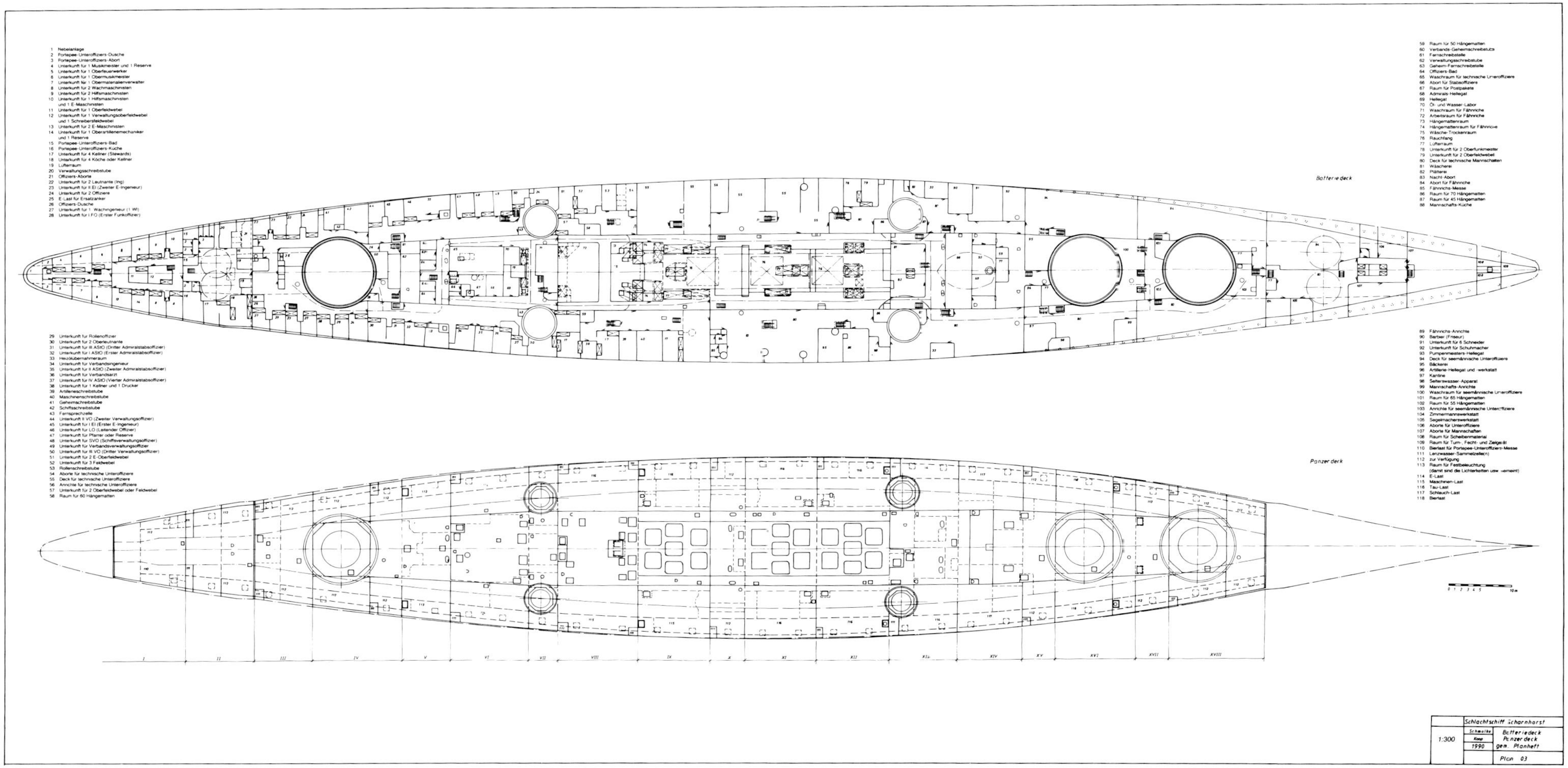
1 Nebelanlage
2 Portepee-Unteroffiziers-Dusche
3 Portepee-Unteroffiziers-Abort
4 Unterkunft für 1 Musikmeister und 1 Reserve
5 Unterkunft für 1 Oberfeuerwerker
6 Unterkunft für 1 Obermusikmeister
7 Unterkunft für 1 Obermaterialienverwalter
8 Unterkunft für 2 Wachmaschinisten
9 Unterkunft für 2 Hilfsmaschinisten
10 Unterkunft für 1 Hilfsmaschinisten und 1 E-Maschinisten
11 Unterkunft für 1 Oberfeldwebel
12 Unterkunft für 1 Verwaltungsoberfeldwebel und 1 Schreibersfeldwebel
13 Unterkunft für 2 E-Maschinisten
14 Unterkunft für 1 Oberartilleriemechaniker und 1 Reserve
15 Portepee-Unteroffiziers-Bad
16 Portepee-Unteroffiziers-Küche
17 Unterkunft für 4 Kellner (Stewards)
18 Unterkunft für 4 Köche oder Kellner
19 Lüfterraum
20 Verwaltungsschreibstube
21 Offiziers-Aborte
22 Unterkunft für 2 Leutnante (Ing)
23 Unterkunft für II.EI (Zweiter E-Ingenieur)
24 Unterkunft für 2 Offiziere
25 E-Last für Ersatzanker
26 Offiziers-Dusche
27 Unterkunft für 1. Wachingenieur (1. WI)
28 Unterkunft für I.FO (Erster Funkoffizier)
29 Unterkunft für Rollenoffizier
30 Unterkunft für 2 Oberleutnante
31 Unterkunft für III.AStO (Dritter Admiralstabsoffizier)
32 Unterkunft für I.AStO (Erster Admiralstabsoffizier)
33 Heizölübernahmeraum
34 Unterkunft für Verbandsingenieur
35 Unterkunft für II AStO (Zweiter Admiralstabsoffizier)
36 Unterkunft für Verbandsarzt
37 Unterkunft für IV.AStO (Vierter Admiralstabsoffizier)
38 Unterkunft für 1 Kellner und 1 Drucker
39 Artillerieschreibstube
40 Maschinenschreibstube
41 Geheimschreibstube
42 Schiffsschreibstube
43 Fernsprechzelle
44 Unterkunft II VO (Zweiter Verwaltungsoffizier)
45 Unterkunft für I EI (Erster E-Ingenieur)
46 Unterkunft für LO (Leitender Offizier)
47 Unterkunft für Pfarrer oder Reserve
48 Unterkunft für SVO (Schiffsverwaltungsoffizier)
49 Unterkunft für Verbandsverwaltungsoffizier
50 Unterkunft für III.VO (Dritter Verwaltungsoffizier)
51 Unterkunft für 2 E-Oberfeldwebel
52 Unterkunft für 3 Feldwebel
53 Rollenschreibstube
54 Aborte für technische Unteroffiziere
55 Deck für technische Unteroffiziere
56 Anrichte für technische Unteroffiziere
57 Unterkunft für 2 Oberfeldwebel oder Feldwebel
58 Raum für 60 Hängematten
59 Raum für 50 Hängematten
60 Verbands-Geheimschreibstube
61 Fernschreibstelle
62 Verwaltungsschreibstube
63 Geheim-Fernschreibstelle
64 Offiziers-Bad
65 Waschraum für technische Unteroffiziere
66 Abort für Stabsoffiziere
67 Raum für Postpakete
68 Admirals-Hellegat
69 Hellegat
70 Öl- und Wasser-Labor
71 Waschraum für Fähnriche
72 Arbeitsraum für Fähnriche
73 Hängemattenraum
74 Hängemattenraum für Fähnriche
75 Wäsche-Trockenraum
76 Rauchfang
77 Lüfterraum
78 Unterkunft für 2 Oberfunkmeister
79 Unterkunft für 2 Oberfeldwebel
80 Deck für technische Mannschaften
81 Wäscherei
82 Plätterei
83 Nacht-Abort
84 Abort für Fähnriche
85 Fähnrichs-Messe
86 Raum für 70 Hängematten
87 Raum für 45 Hängematten
88 Mannschafts-Küche
89 Fähnrichs-Anrichte
90 Barbier (Friseur)
91 Unterkunft für 6 Schneider
92 Unterkunft für Schuhmacher
93 Pumpenmeisters-Hellegat
94 Deck für seemännische Unteroffiziere
95 Bäckerei
96 Artillerie-Hellegat und -werkstatt
97 Kantine
98 Selterswasser-Apparat
99 Mannschafts-Anrichte
100 Waschraum für seemännische Unteroffiziere
101 Raum für 65 Hängematten
102 Raum für 55 Hängematten
103 Anrichte für seemännische Unteroffiziere
104 Zimmermannswerkstatt
105 Segelmacherswerkstatt
106 Aborte für Unteroffiziere
107 Aborte für Mannschaften
108 Raum für Scheibenmaterial
109 Raum für Turn-, Fecht- und Zielgerät
110 Bierlast für Portepee-Unteroffiziers-Messe
111 Lenzwasser-Sammelzelle(n)
112 zur Verfügung
113 Raum für Festbeleuchtung (damit sind die Lichterketten usw. gemeint)
114 E-Last
115 Maschinen-Last
116 Tau-Last
117 Schlauch-Last
118 Bierlast
Batteriedeck
Panzerdeck
Schlachtschiff Scharnhorst
1:300
Batteriedeck
Panzerdeck
gem. Planheft
1990
Plan 03

Plan 04

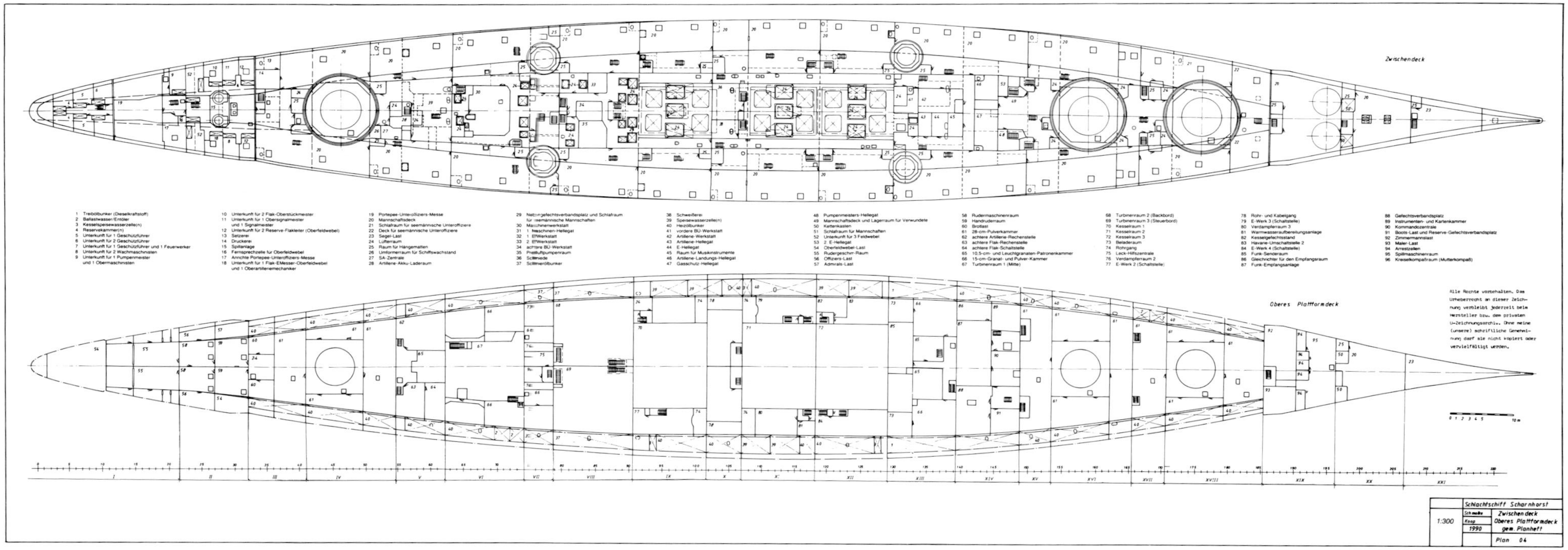

Zwischendeck
Oberes Plattformdeck
1 Treibölbunker (Dieselkraftstoff)
2 Ballastwasser/Entöler
3 Kesselspeisewasserzelle(n)
4 Reservekammer(n)
5 Unterkunft für 1 Geschützführer
6 Unterkunft für 2 Geschützführer
7 Unterkunft für 1 Geschützführer und 1 Feuerwerker
8 Unterkunft für 2 Wachmaschinisten
9 Unterkunft für 1 Pumpenmeister und 1 Obermaschinisten
10 Unterkunft für 2 Flak-Oberstückmeister
11 Unterkunft für 1 Obersignalmeister und 1 Signalmeister
12 Unterkunft für 2 Reserve-Flakleiter (Oberfeldwebel)
13 Setzerei
14 Druckerei
15 Spillanlage
16 Fernsprechzelle für Oberfeldwebel
17 Anrichte Portepee-Unteroffiziers-Messe
18 Unterkunft für 1 Flak-EMesser-Oberfeldwebel und 1 Oberartilleriemechaniker
19 Portepee-Unteroffiziers-Messe
20 Mannschaftsdeck
21 Schlafraum für seemännische Unteroffiziere
22 Deck für seemännische Unteroffiziere
23 Segel-Last
24 Lüfterraum
25 Raum für Hängematten
26 Umformerraum für Schiffswachstand
27 SA-Zentrale
28 Artillerie-Akku-Laderaum
29 Nebengefechtsverbandsplatz und Schlafraum für seemännische Mannschaften
30 Maschinenwerkstatt
31 1. Maschinen-Hellegat
32 1. E-Werkstatt
33 2. E-Werkstatt
34 achtere BÜ-Werkstatt
35 Preßluftpumpenraum
36 Schmiede
37 Schmierölbunker
38 Schweißerei
39 Speisewasserzelle(n)
40 Heizölbunker
41 vordere BÜ-Werkstatt
42 Artillerie-Werkstatt
43 Artillerie-Hellegat
44 E-Hellegat
45 Raum für Musikinstrumente
46 Artillerie-Landungs-Hellegat
47 Gasschutz-Hellegat
48 Pumpenmeisters-Hellegat
49 Mannschaftsdeck und Lagerraum für Verwundete
50 Kettenkasten
51 Schlafraum für Mannschaften
52 Unterkunft für 3 Feldwebel
53 2. E-Hellegat
54 Oberfeldwebel-Last
55 Rudergeschirr-Raum
56 Offiziers-Last
57 Admirals-Last
58 Rudermaschinenraum
59 Handruderraum
60 Brotlast
61 28-cm-Pulverkammer
62 achtere Artillerie-Rechenstelle
63 achtere Flak-Rechenstelle
64 achtere Flak-Schaltstelle
65 10,5-cm- und Leuchtgranaten-Patronenkammer
66 15-cm-Granat- und Pulver-Kammer
67 Turbinenraum 1 (Mitte)
68 Turbinenraum 2 (Backbord)
69 Turbinenraum 3 (Steuerbord)
70 Kesselraum 1
71 Kesselraum 2
72 Kesselraum 3
73 Beladeraum
74 Rohrgang
75 Leck-Hilfszentrale
76 Verdampferraum 2
77 E-Werk 2 (Schaltstelle)
78 Rohr- und Kabelgang
79 E-Werk 3 (Schaltstelle)
80 Verdampferraum 3
81 Warmwasseraufbereitungsanlage
82 Kesselgefechtsstand
83 Havarie-Umschaltstelle 2
84 E-Werk 4 (Schaltstelle)
85 Funk-Senderaum
86 Gleichrichter für den Empfangsraum
87 Funk-Empfangsanlage
88 Gefechtsverbandsplatz
89 Instrumenten- und Kartenkammer
90 Kommandozentrale
91 Boots-Last und Reserve-Gefechtsverbandsplatz
92 Zimmermannslast
93 Maler-Last
94 Arrestzellen
95 Spillmaschinenraum
96 Kreiselkompaßraum (Mutterkompaß)
Alle Rechte vorbehalten. Das Urheberrecht an dieser Zeichnung verbleibt jederzeit beim Hersteller bzw. dem privaten U-Zeichnungsarchiv. Ohne meine (unsere) schriftliche Genehmigung darf sie nicht kopiert oder vervielfältigt werden.
0 1 2 3 4 5 10 m
Schlachtschiff Scharnhorst
1:300
Schmolke
Koop
1990
Zwischendeck
Oberes Plattformdeck
gem. Planheft
Plan 04

Plan 05

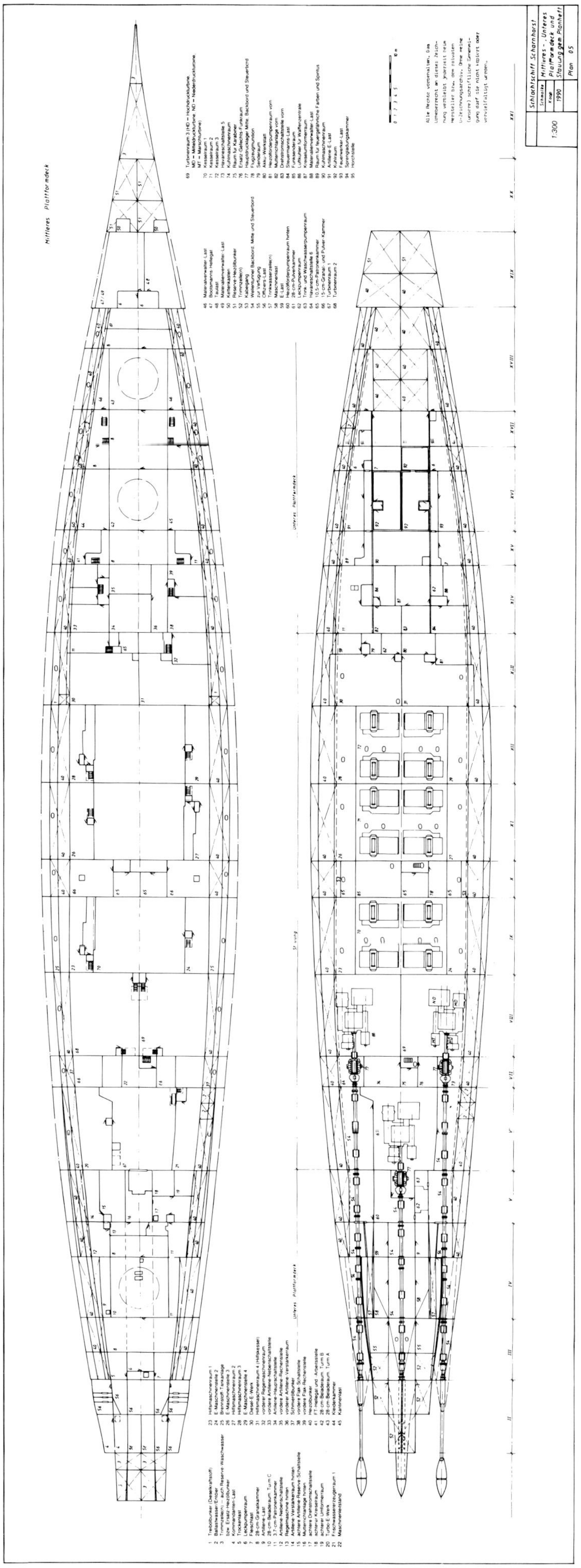

Mittleres Plattformdeck
Unteres Plattformdeck
Schlachtschiff Scharnhorst
1:300
1990
Plan 05

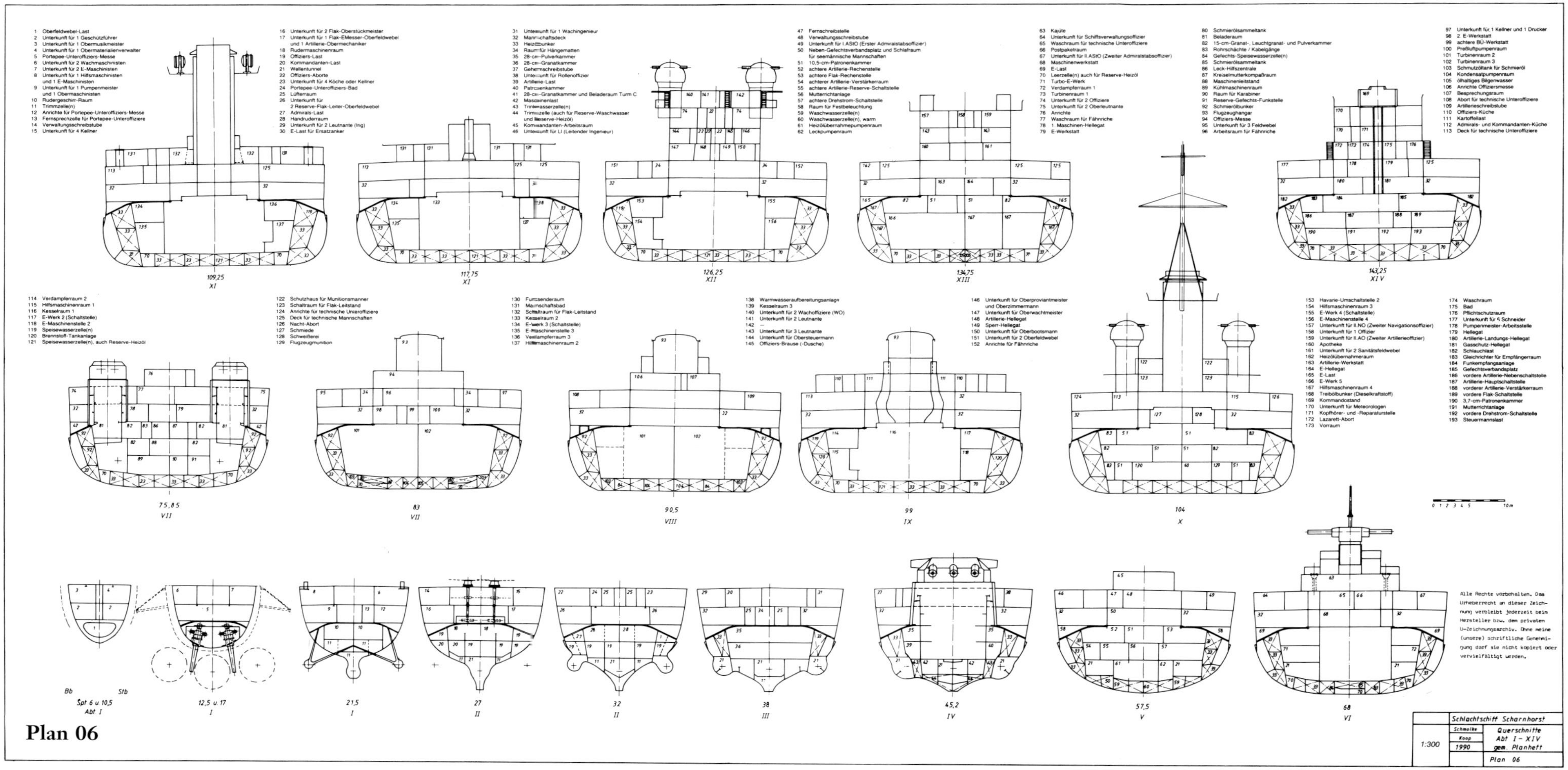

Plan 06

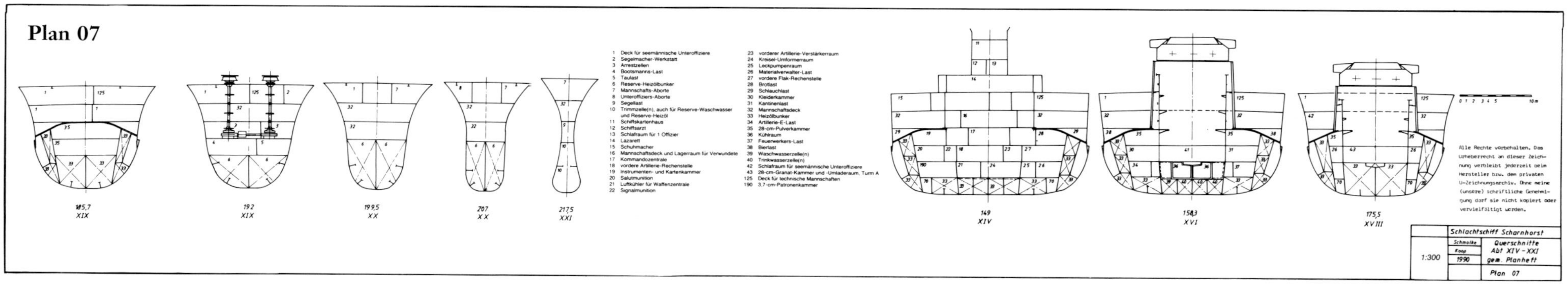

Plan 07

Plan 08

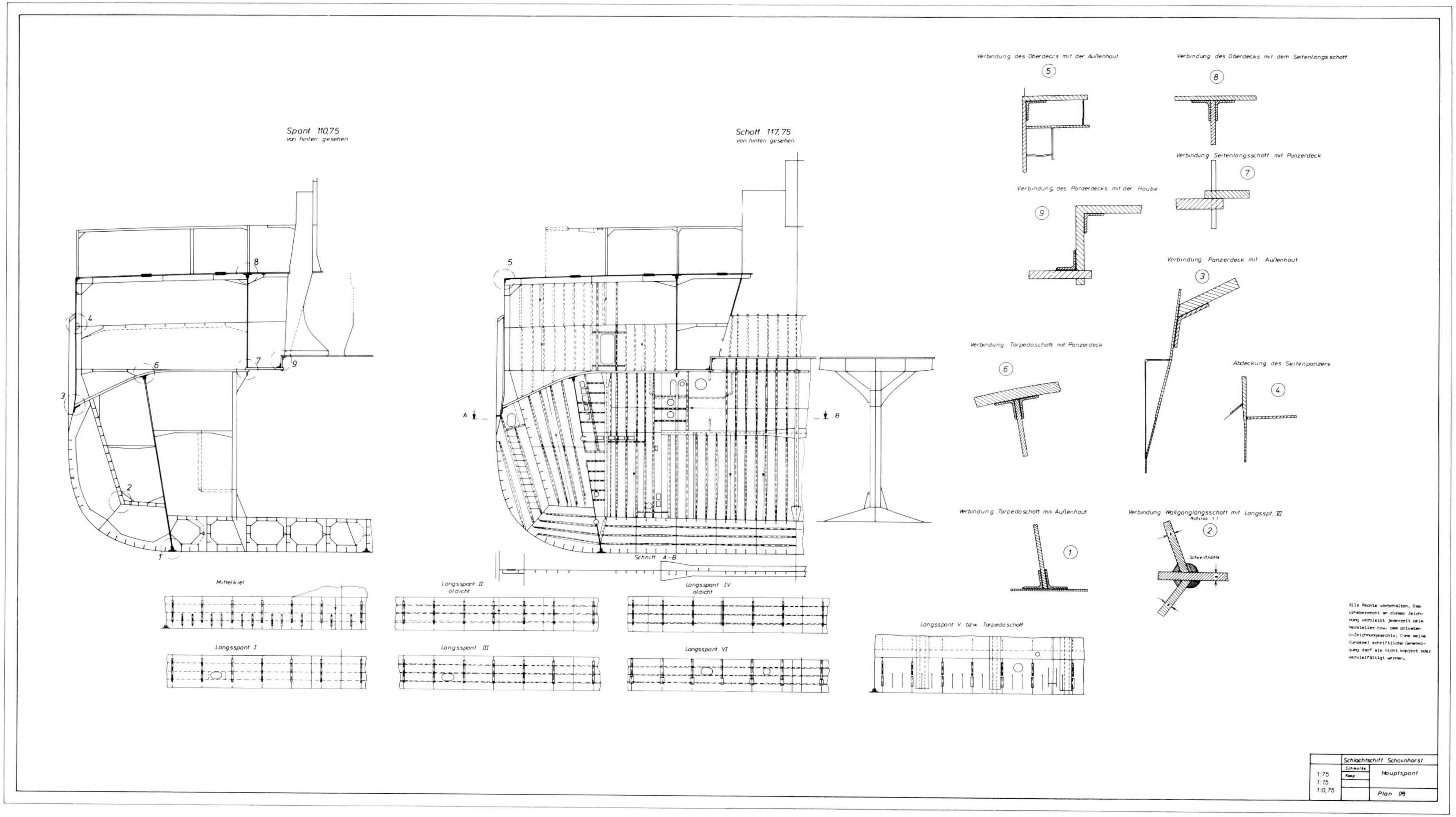
Spant 110,75
von hinten gesehen
Schott 117,75
von hinten gesehen
Schnitt A-B
Mittelkiel
Langsspant I
Langsspant II
öldicht
Langsspant III
Langsspant IV
öldicht
Langsspant VI
Langsspant V bzw Torpedoschott
Verbindung des Oberdecks mit der Außenhaut
Verbindung des Oberdecks mit dem Seitenlangsschott
Verbindung Seitenlangsschott mit Panzerdeck
Verbindung des Panzerdecks mit der Haube
Verbindung Panzerdeck mit Außenhaut
Verbindung Torpedoschott mit Panzerdeck
Abdeckung des Seitenpanzers
Verbindung Torpedoschott mit Außenhaut
Verbindung Wallganglangsschott mit Langsspt. VI
Maßstab 1:1
Schweißnähte
Alle Rechte vorbehalten. Das Urheberrecht an dieser Zeichnung verbleibt jederzeit beim Hersteller bzw. dem privaten U-Zeichnungsarchiv. Ohne meine (unsere) schriftliche Genehmigung darf sie nicht kopiert oder vervielfältigt werden.
Schlachtschiff Scharnhorst
1:75
1:15
1:0,75
Schmolke
Koop
Hauptspant
Plan 08

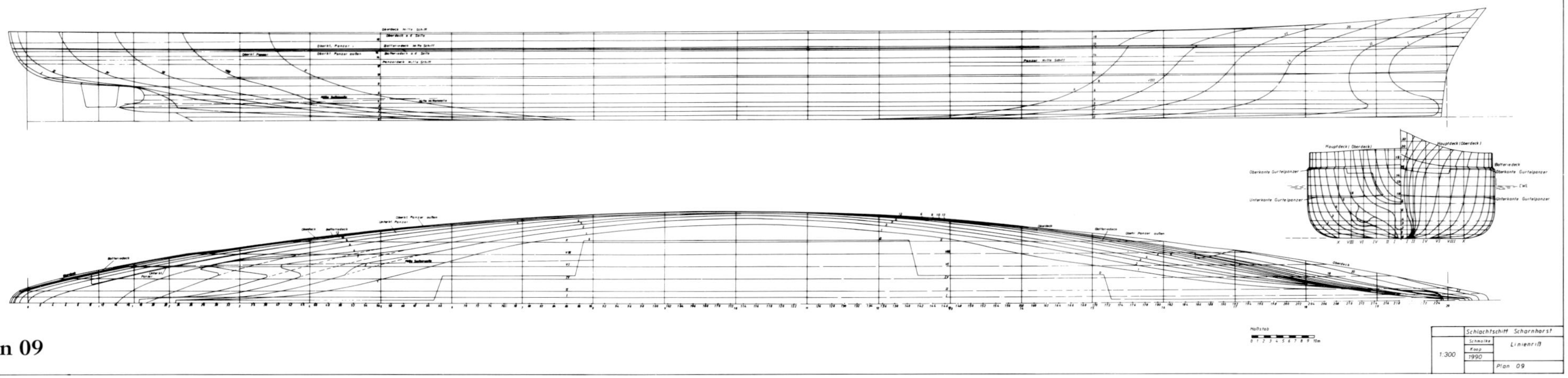

Plan 09

Plan 10

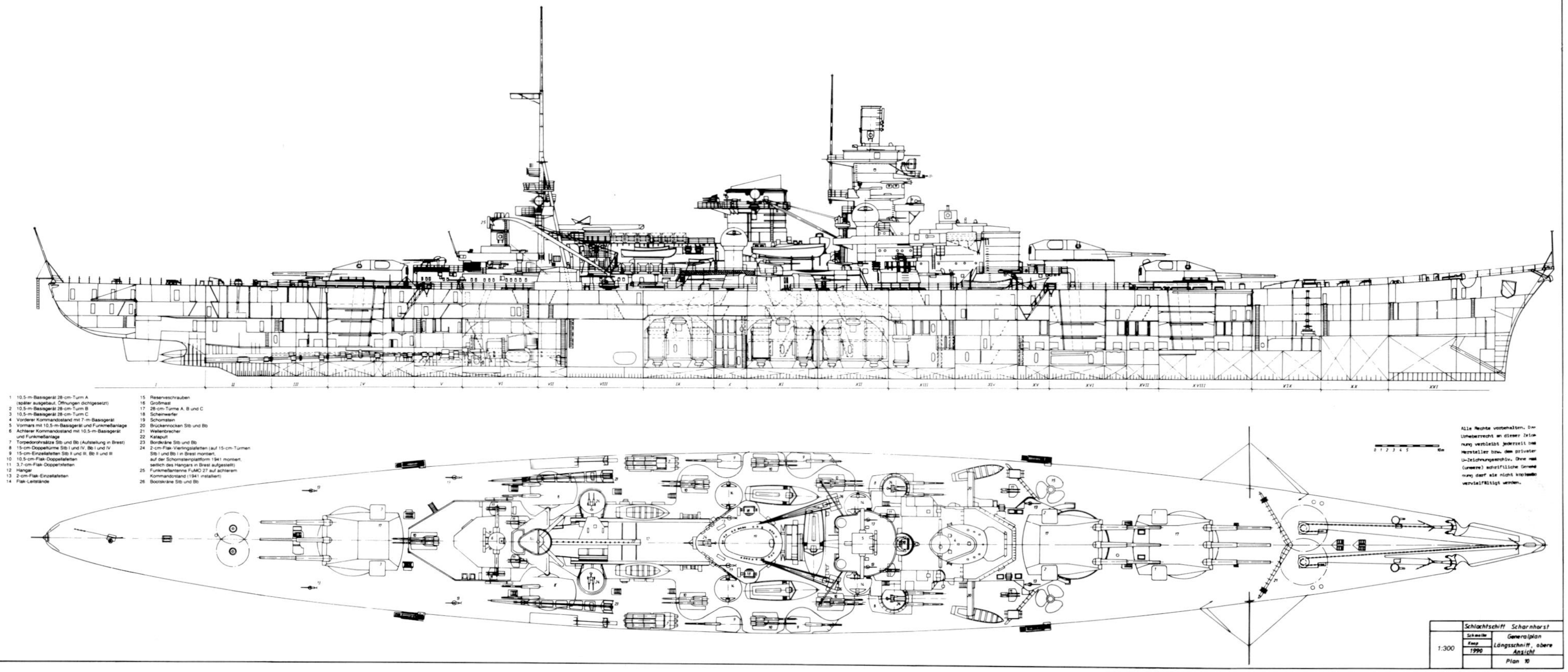

Plan 11

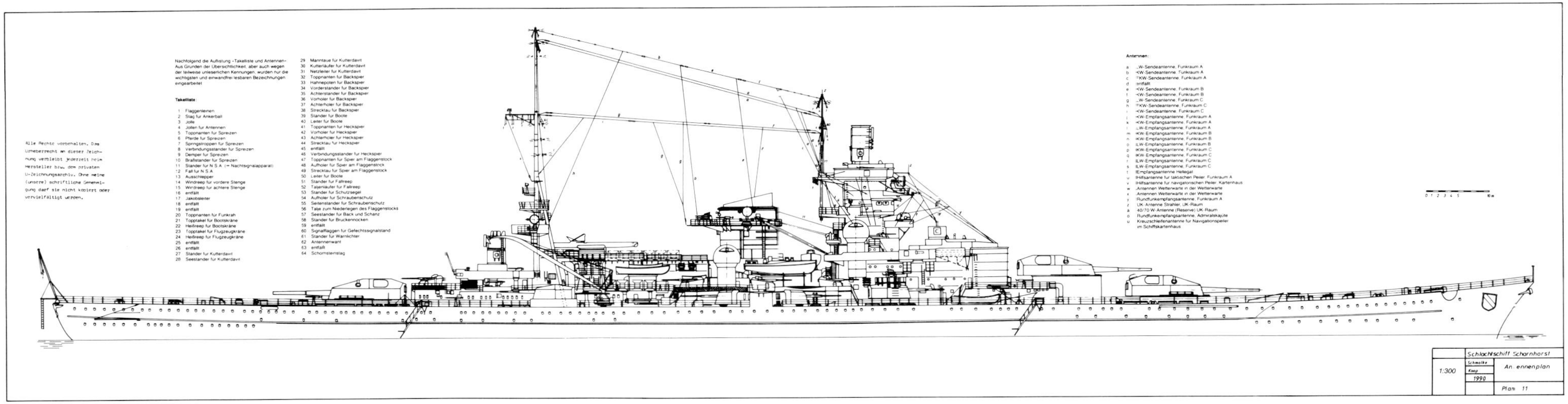
Alle Rechte vorbehalten. Das Urheberrecht an dieser Zeichnung verbleibt jederzeit beim Hersteller bzw. dem privaten U-Zeichnungsarchiv. Ohne meine (unsere) schriftliche Genehmigung darf sie nicht kopiert oder vervielfältigt werden.
Nachfolgend die Auflistung »Takelliste und Antennen«. Aus Gründen der Übersichtlichkeit, aber auch wegen der teilweise unleserlichen Kennungen, wurden nur die wichtigsten und einwandfrei lesbaren Bezeichnungen eingearbeitet.
Takelliste:
1 Flaggenleinen
2 Stag für Ankerball
3 Jolle
4 Jollen für Antennen
5 Toppnanten für Spreizen
6 Pferde für Spreizen
7 Springstroppen für Spreizen
8 Verbindungsstander für Spreizen
9 Demper für Spreizen
10 Braßstander für Spreizen
11 Stander für N.S.A. (= Nachtsignalapparat)
12 Fall für N.S.A.
13 Ausschlepper
14 Windreep für vordere Stenge
15 Windreep für achtere Stenge
16 entfällt
17 Jakobsleiter
18 entfällt
19 entfällt
20 Toppnanten für Funkrah
21 Topptakel für Bootskräne
22 Heißreep für Bootskräne
23 Topptakel für Flugzeugkräne
24 Heißreep für Flugzeugkräne
25 entfällt
26 entfällt
27 Stander für Kutterdavit
28 Seestander für Kutterdavit
29 Manntaue für Kutterdavit
30 Kutterläufer für Kutterdavit
31 Netzleiter für Kutterdavit
32 Toppnanten für Backspier
33 Hahnepoten für Backspier
34 Vorderstander für Backspier
35 Achterstander für Backspier
36 Vorholer für Backspier
37 Achterholer für Backspier
38 Strecktau für Backspier
39 Stander für Boote
40 Leiter für Boote
41 Toppnanten für Heckspier
42 Vorholer für Heckspier
43 Achterholer für Heckspier
44 Strecktau für Heckspier
45 entfällt
46 Verbindungsstander für Heckspier
47 Toppnanten für Spier am Flaggenstock
48 Aufholer für Spier am Flaggenstock
49 Strecktau für Spier am Flaggenstock
50 Leiter für Boote
51 Stander für Fallreep
52 Taljenläufer für Fallreep
53 Stander für Schutzsegel
54 Aufholer für Schraubenschutz
55 Seitenstander für Schraubenschutz
56 Talje zum Niederlegen des Flaggenstocks
57 Seestander für Back und Schanz
58 Stander für Brückennocken
59 entfällt
60 Signalflaggen für Gefechtssignalstand
61 Stander für Warnlichter
62 Antennenwant
63 entfällt
64 Schornsteinstag
Antennen:
a W-Sendeantenne, Funkraum A
b KW-Sendeantenne, Funkraum A
c KW-Sendeantenne, Funkraum A
d entfällt
e KW-Sendeantenne, Funkraum B
f KW-Sendeantenne, Funkraum B
g W-Sendeantenne, Funkraum C
h KW-Sendeantenne, Funkraum C
i KW-Sendeantenne, Funkraum C
j KW-Empfangsantenne, Funkraum A
k KW-Empfangsantenne, Funkraum A
l LW-Empfangsantenne, Funkraum A
m KW-Empfangsantenne, Funkraum B
n KW-Empfangsantenne, Funkraum B
o LW-Empfangsantenne, Funkraum B
p KW-Empfangsantenne, Funkraum C
q KW-Empfangsantenne, Funkraum C
r LW-Empfangsantenne, Funkraum C
s LW-Empfangsantenne, Funkraum C
t Empfangsantenne Hellegat
u Hilfsantenne für taktischen Peiler, Funkraum A
v Hilfsantenne für navigatorischen Peiler, Kartenhaus
w Antennen Wetterwarte in der Wetterwarte
x Antennen Wetterwarte in der Wetterwarte
y Rundfunkempfangsantenne, Funkraum A
z UK-Antenne Strahler, UK-Raum
ä 40/70 W-Antenne (Reserve) UK-Raum
ö Rundfunkempfangsantenne, Admiralskajüte
ü Kreuzschleifenantenne für Navigationspeiler im Schiffskartenhaus
0 1 2 3 4 5 10 m
Schlachtschiff Scharnhorst
1:300
Schmolke
Koop
1990
An.ennenplan
Plan 11

Plan 12

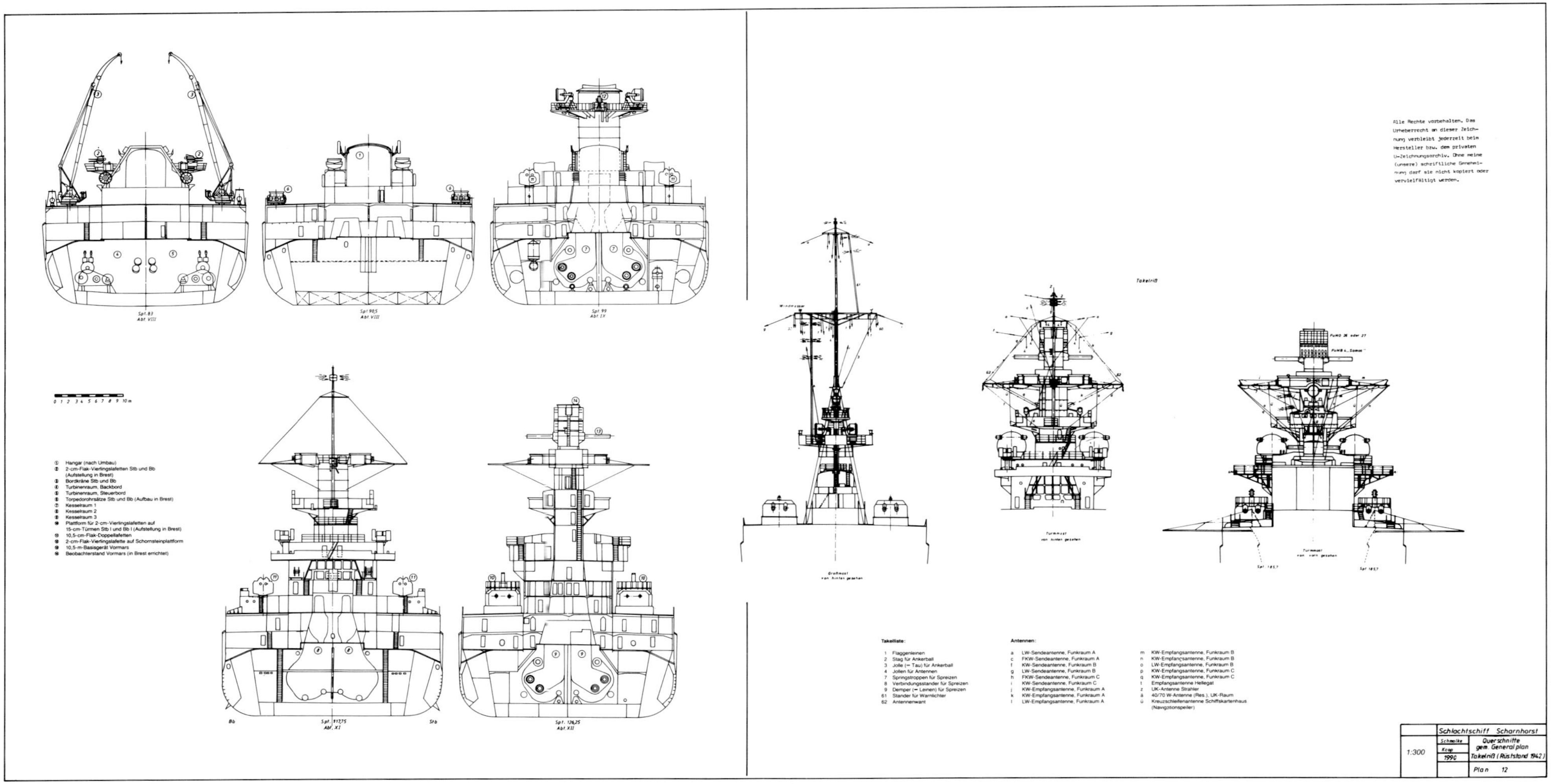

Spt. 83
Abt. VIII
Spt. 98,5
Abt. VIII
Spt. 99
Abt. IX
0 1 2 3 4 5 6 7 8 9 10 m
① Hangar (nach Umbau)
② 2-cm-Flak-Vierlingslafetten Stb und Bb (Aufstellung in Brest)
③ Bordkräne Stb und Bb
④ Turbinenraum, Backbord
⑤ Turbinenraum, Steuerbord
⑥ Torpedorohrsätze Stb und Bb (Aufbau in Brest)
⑦ Kesselraum 1
⑧ Kesselraum 2
⑨ Kesselraum 3
⑩ Plattform für 2-cm-Vierlingslafetten auf 15-cm-Türmen Stb I und Bb I (Aufstellung in Brest)
⑪ 10,5-cm-Flak-Doppellafetten
⑫ 2-cm-Flak-Vierlingslafette auf Schornsteinplattform
⑬ 10,5-m-Basisgerät Vormars
⑭ Beobachterstand Vormars (in Brest errichtet)
Bb
Spt. 117,75
Abt. XI
Stb
Spt. 126,25
Abt. XII
Takelriß
Takelliste:
1 Flaggenleinen
2 Stag für Ankerball
3 Jolle (= Tau) für Ankerball
4 Jollen für Antennen
7 Springstroppen für Spreizen
8 Verbindungsstander für Spreizen
9 Demper (= Leinen) für Spreizen
61 Stander für Warnlichter
62 Antennenwant
Antennen:
a LW-Sendeantenne, Funkraum A
c FKW-Sendeantenne, Funkraum A
f KW-Sendeantenne, Funkraum B
g LW-Sendeantenne, Funkraum B
h FKW-Sendeantenne, Funkraum C
i KW-Sendeantenne, Funkraum C
j KW-Empfangsantenne, Funkraum A
k KW-Empfangsantenne, Funkraum A
l LW-Empfangsantenne, Funkraum A
m KW-Empfangsantenne, Funkraum B
n KW-Empfangsantenne, Funkraum B
o LW-Empfangsantenne, Funkraum B
p KW-Empfangsantenne, Funkraum C
q KW-Empfangsantenne, Funkraum C
t Empfangsantenne Hellegat
z UK-Antenne Strahler
ä 40/70 W-Antenne (Res.), UK-Raum
ü Kreuzschleifenantenne Schiffskartenhaus (Navigationspeiler)
Alle Rechte vorbehalten. Das Urheberrecht an dieser Zeichnung verbleibt jederzeit beim Hersteller bzw. dem privaten U-Zeichnungsarchiv. Ohne meine (unsere) schriftliche Genehmigung darf sie nicht kopiert oder vervielfältigt werden.
Schlachtschiff Scharnhorst
Schmalke
Krap
1990
Querschnitte gem. Generalplan
Takelriß (Rüststand 1942)
1:300
Plan 12

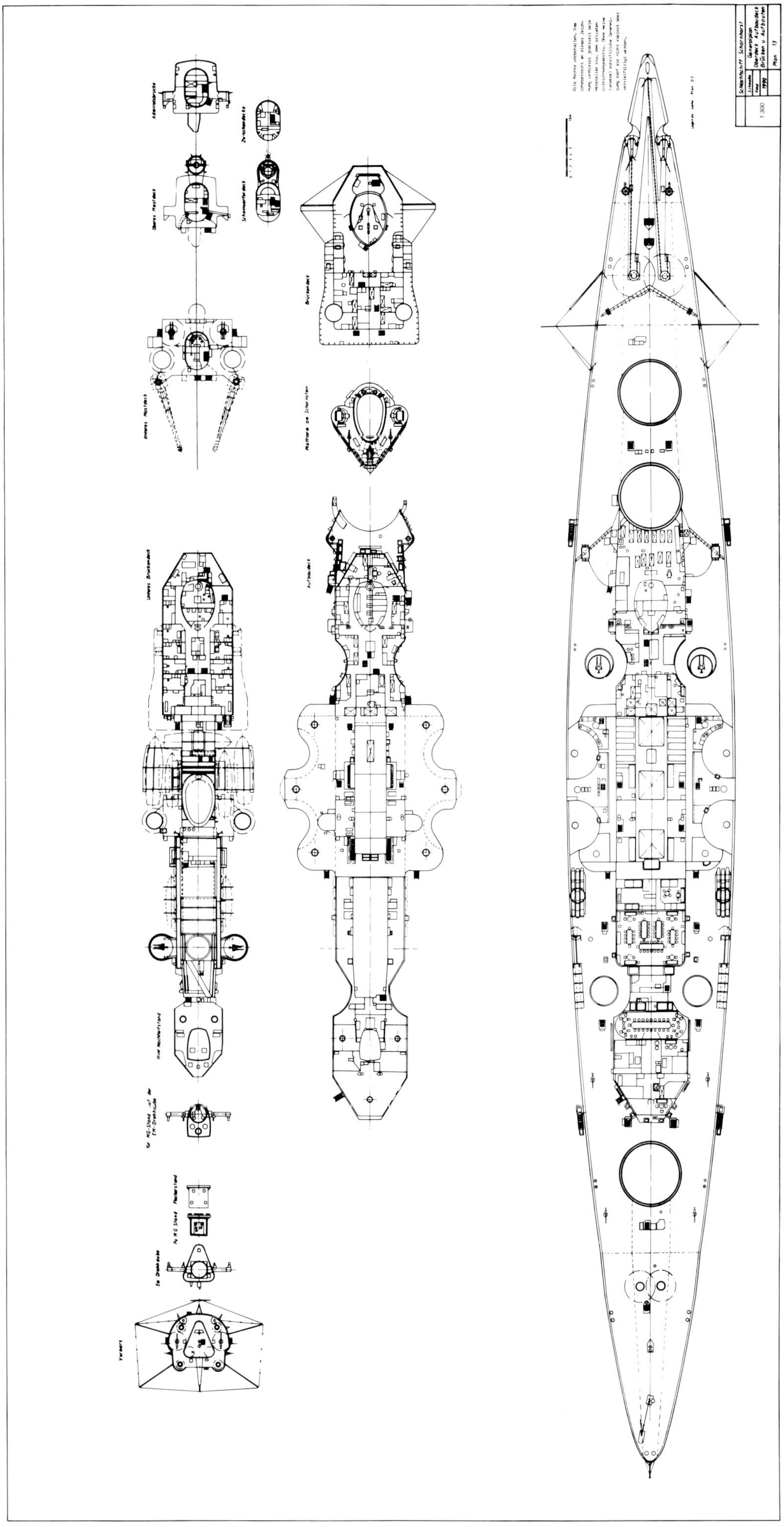

Plan 13

Plan Keys

PLAN 01

1 28cm turret A
2 28cm turret B
3 28cm turret C
4 15cm turret, starboard 1
5 15cm turret, starboard 2
6 15cm gun, single mounting, starboard 1
7 15cm gun, single mounting, starboard 2
8 10.5cm guns, twin mounting, starboard and amidships
9 fore conning tower with 6m base rangefinder
10 aft conning tower with 10.5m base rangefinder
11 AA directors SL 6, starboard and amidships
12 10.5m base rangefinders in 28cm turrets A, B and C (later removed from A)
13 main artillery director control tower in the foretop with 10.5m base rangefinder
14 searchlight
15 catapult, central
16 catapult on turret C (later removed)
17 aircraft hangar (later removed)
18 crane, starboard, for boats
19 capstan, bow, starboard
20 jack staff
21 stern flag staff
22 aft capstan, starboard
23 stern flag staff
24 2cm AA guns, single mountings
25 3.7cm AA guns, twin mountings
26 hawse for stern anchor, port
27 rear side hawse, bow, port
28 extension drive, paravane
29 main mast with telescopic top (later moved aft)
30 ballast
31 trim tanks(s)
32 trim tanks, also for reserve washing water
33 fresh water tank(s)
34 washing water tank(s)
35 lubrication oil collecting tank(s)
36 feed tank(s)
37 lubrication oil tank
38 oil-polluted bilge water (tanks)
39 feed tank
40 oil fuel tank
41 evaporation room
42 speedometer
43 oil fuel tank, reserve
44 boom, starboard and port
45 propeller protectors, starboard and port
46 gangways, starboard and port
47 15cm turret, port 1
48 15cm turret, port 2
49 15cm gun, single mounting, port 1
50 15cm gun, single mounting, port 2
51 10.5cm twin mountings, port
52 crane, port, for boats
53 AA directors SL 6, port
54 cranes, port and starboard, for aircraft
55 crane for aircraft on turret C (later removed)
56 cutter
57 traffic boats
58 motor launch
59 motor pinnace
60 motor boats
61 funnel
62 bridge tower
63 capstan, bow, port
64 capstan, stern, port
65 breakwater

PLAN 02

1 officer's WC
2 admiral's bridge cabin
3 communications centre
4 communications centre
5 charthouse
6 switchboard
7 shelter
8 cabin for 2 officers
9 cabin for military judge
19 cabin for I.NO (chief signal officer)
11 cabin for II.NO (2nd signal officer)
12 cabin for meteorological officer
13 cabin for military court secretary
14 charthouse
15 transmitter room
16 officer's bath
17 officer's cabin (III. artillery officer)
18 officer's cabin (II. artillery officer)
19 officer's cabin (chief artillery officer)
20 officer's cabin (1 officer)
21 signal bridge
22 watch officer's cabin (1 officer)
23 watch officer's cabin (2 officers)
24 cabin for 2 lieutenants
25 cabin for 3 lieutenants
26 shelter for signalmen
27 cabin for ATO
28 captain's cabin
29 fore director control tower
30 conning tower
31 shelter
32 3.7cm AA guns
33 meteorological office
34 radar office
35 10.5cm AA guns
36 2-cm AA guns
37 aircraft hangar
38 vent
39 shelter for gunners
40 chief petty officer's cabin
41 deputy surgeon's cabin
42 surgeon's cabin
43 executive officer's cabin
44 2nd deputy surgeon's cabin
45 cabin for catering officer and carpenter
46 protective clothing store
47 officer's showers
48 radio repair shop
49 captain's office
50 captain's cabin
51 captain's bathroom
52 flag lieutenant's cabin
53 adjutant's cabin
54 admiral's bathroom
55 admiral's cabin
56 admiral's office
57 cabin
58 ante-room
59 pantry
60 ante-room
61 wardroom
62 pantry
63 conference room
64 officer's galley
65 potato store
66 admiral's/captain's galley
67 seamen's bathroom
68 switchboard room for AA director control tower
69 motorboat equipment store
70 lamp store
71 vegetable store
72 SNCO's cabin
73 petty officer's office
74 medical NCO's cabin
75 SNCO's cabin
76 storeroom
77 artillery store room
78 shelter room
79 hospital store room
80 launderette
81 bathroom
82 X-ray room
83 hospital
84 operation theatre
85 ante-room hospital
86 WC, hospital
87 isolation ward

PLAN 03

1 fog generator
2 SNCO's showers
3 SNCO's WC
4 bandleader's cabin
5 pyrotechnical SNCO's cabin
6 chief bandleader's cabin
7 chief quartermaster SNCO's cabin
8 engineer SNCO's cabin (2nd SNCO)
9 engineer's cabin
10 engineer's cabin
11 SNCO's cabin
12 admin SNCO'S and chief clerk's cabin
13 engineer's cabin
14 artillery SNCO's cabin
15 SNCO's bathroom
16 SNCO's galley
17 mess steward's cabin (4)
18 cook's cabin (4)
19 ventilation room
20 office
21 officer's WC
22 officer's cabin (2 lieutenants)
23 engineer officer's cabin
24 officer's cabin
25 electrical spare parts store
26 officer's showers
27 engineer officer's cabin
28 signal officer's cabin
29 station officer's cabin
30 officer's cabin (2 first lieutenants)
31 admiral staff officer's cabin
32 admiral staff officer's cabin
33 oil fuel transfer room
34 engineer's cabin
35 admiral staff officer's cabin
36 fleet surgeon's cabin
37 admiral staff officer's cabin
38 cabin for mess steward/printer
39 artillery administration office
40 machinery administration office
41 crypto office
42 chief clerk's office
43 telephone box
44 admin offer's cabin
45 engineer officer's cabin
46 chief engineer officer's cabin
47 chaplain's cabin
48 admin officer's cabin
49 fleet admin officer's cabin
50 admin officer's cabin
51 SNCO's cabin (2)
52 SNCO's cabin (3)
53 admin office
54 engineer NCO's WC
55 engineer NCO'S restroom
56 engineer NCO'S pantry
57 SNCO's cabin
58 hammock store (60 hammocks)
59 hammock store (50 hammocks)
60 fleet crypto office
61 communications centre
62 admin office
63 commcen, protected lines
64 officer's bathroom
65 engineer NCO's launderette
66 senior officer's WC
67 post office store room
68 admiral's store room
69 store room
70 oil and water laboratory
71 ensign's launderette
72 ensign's workroom
73 hammock store
74 hammock store, ensigns
75 drying room for washing
76 smoke collector
77 ventilation
78 signal SNCO's cabin
79 SNCO's cabin
80 engineer's deck
81 laundry
82 steam laundry
83 night WC
84 ensign's WC
85 ensign's mess
86 hammock store (70 hammocks)
87 hammock store (45 hammocks)
88 seamen's galley
89 ensign's pantry
90 barber shop
91 cabin for 6 tailors
92 shoemaker's cabin
93 pumpmaster's store
94 NCO's deck
95 bakery
96 artillery store
97 canteen
98 mineral water fountain
99 seamen's pantry
100 NCO's launderette
101 hammock store (65 hammocks)
102 hammock store (55 hammocks)
103 NCO's pantry
104 carpenter's workshop
105 sailmaker's workshop
106 NCO's WC
107 seamen's heads
108 target store
109 sports equipment store
110 beer store for petty officer's mess
111 bilge tank
112 spare store room
113 lamp store
114 electrical store
115 spare parts store
116 rope store
117 hosepipe store
118 beer storage

PLAN 04

1 diesel tank
2 ballast tank
3 feed tank
4 reserve cabins
5 cabin for 1 gun commander
6 cabin for 2 gun commanders
7 cabin for 1 gun commander and 1 fireworker
8 cabin for 2 engineers
9 cabin for 1 pump master and 1 engineer SNCO
10 cabin for 2 AA gunnery SNCOs
11 cabin for 1 signal SNCO and 1 signal NCO
12 cabin for two reserve AA fire control SNCOs
13 typesetting room
14 printers
15 spill gear
16 telephone box for SNCOs
17 pantry SNCO's mess
18 cabin for one AA fire control SNCO and one artillery SNCO
19 SNCO's mess
20 seamen's deck
21 sleeping room for NCOs
22 NCO's deck
23 sailmaker's store
24 ventilation room
25 hammock store
26 electrical power conversion room
27 heavy artillery fire control centre
28 battery charging room
29 dressing station and seamen's sleeping room
30 engineer workshop
31 workshop storeroom
32 electrical engineering workshop No 1
33 electrical engineering workshop No 2
34 aft engineer workshop
35 compressed air pumping room
36 forge
37 lubrication oil tank
38 welding shop
39 feed tanks
40 oil fuel tanks
41 fore engineer workshop
42 artillery workshop
43 artillery store
44 electrical store
45 musical instruments store
46 landing party artillery store
47 gas protection store
48 pumpmaster's store
49 seamen's deck and reserve hospital
50 chain room
51 seamen's sleeping room
52 cabin for 3 SNCOs
53 2nd electrical store
54 ballast
55 steering gear storeroom
56 officer's storeroom
57 admiral's storeroom
58 steering gear compartment
59 manual steering room
60 bread store
61 28cm magazine
62 aft artillery fire control room
63 aft AA fire control room
64 aft AA power control room
65 10.5cm and illumination shell magazine
66 15cm magazine
67 turbine room No 1 (inner)
68 turbine room No 2 (port)
69 turbine room No 3 (starboard)
70 boiler room No 1
71 boiler room No 2
72 boiler room No 3
73 storeroom
74 tube walkway
75 auxiliary damage control centre
76 evaporator room No 2
77 power plant No 2
78 tube and cable trunk
79 power plant No 3
80 evaporator room No 3
81 hot water purification plant
82 boiler control centre
83 damage change-over position No 2
84 power plant No 4
85 radio transmission room
86 alternator for radio receiver room
87 radio receiver room
88 dressing station
89 instrument and chart store
90 control centre
91 store room and reserve dressing station
92 carpenter's store
93 painter's store
94 detention cells
95 capstan engine room
96 gyro compass room

PLAN 05

1 diesel tank
2 ballast water
3 trim tank/reserve washing water/reserve oil fuel tank
4 captain's store room
5 drying room
6 pump room
7 meat store
8 28cm shell magazine
9 artillery storeroom
10 28cm transfer station
11 3.7cm magazine
12 artillery reserve switchboard
13 aft regulator room
14 artillery amplification room
15 aft artillery reserve switchboard
16 central artillery training unit
17 aft DC switchboard room
18 aft gyro compass room
19 aft alternator room
20 turbo power plant
21 fresh water generation room No 1
22 machinery control centre
23 auxiliary machinery room No 1
24 electrical machinery station No 2
25 oil fuel bunker control centre
26 electrical machinery station No 3
27 auxiliary machinery room No 2
28 auxiliary machinery room No 3
29 electrical machinery station No 4
30 diesel power plant
31 auxiliary machinery room No 3 (auxiliary boilers)
32 fore regulator room
33 fore artillery reserve switchboard
34 main artillery switchboard
35 fore artillery plotting office
36 fore artillery amplification room
37 lubrication oil tank
38 fore AA switchboard
39 fore AA plotting room
40 oil fuel tank
41 store room
42 28cm transfer station, turret B
43 28cm transfer station, turret A
44 clothing store
45 canteen store
46 quartermaster's store
47 bosun's store
48 rope store
49 quartermaster's store
50 chain room
51 reserve oil fuel tank
52 trim tank
53 cable trunk
54 shaft tunnels, port, starboard and amidships
55 reserve store room
56 officer's store room
57 fresh water tanks
58 engineer store room
59 electrical store room
60 oil fuel pump room, aft
61 28cm magazine
62 leakage pump room
63 fresh water and washing water pump room
64 damage control switchboard No 6
65 10.5cm magazine
66 15cm magazine
67 turbine room No 1
68 turbine room No 2
69 turbine room No 3
70 boiler room No 1
71 boiler room No 2
72 boiler room No 3
73 damage control centre No 5
74 cooling system room
75 small arms store
76 communications centre, reserve
77 main shaft bearings, amidships, port and starboard
78 aircraft ammunition
79 radio transmitter
80 battery workshop
81 oil fuel transfer pumps
82 fore central artillery training unit
83 fore AC switchboard
84 SNCO's store room

85 radio transmitter
86 ventilation and cooling room
87 gyro transmission room
88 quartermaster's store
89 storeroom for inflammable paints and spirit
90 cooling system room
91 artillery electrical spare parts store
92 cool room
93 pyrotechnics store
94 demolition charge chamber
95 sound locator room

PLAN 06

1 SNCO's store room
2 gun commander's cabin
3 chief bandleader's cabin
4 cabin for 1 admin SNCO
5 SNCO's mess
6 cabin for 2 engineers
7 cabin for 2 electrical engineers
8 cabin for 1 engineer and 1 electrical engineer
9 cabin for 1 pumpmaster and 1 engineer SNCO
10 steering gear room
11 trim tank
12 SNCO's mess pantry
13 telephone box for SNCOs
14 chief clerk's office
15 mess steward's cabin (4)
16 cabin for 2 AA gunnery SNCOs
17 cabin for 1 AA rangefinder operation SNCO and 1 artillery engineering SNCO
18 steering gear compartment
19 officer's store room
20 captain's store room
21 shaft tunnel
22 officer's WC
23 cabin for 4 cooks or stewards
24 SNCO's bathroom
25 ventilation room
26 cabin for 2 reserve fire control SNCOs
27 admiral's store room
28 manual steering room
29 cabin for 2 lieutenants (engineers)
30 electrical spare parts store
31 cabin for 1 engineer
32 seamen's deck
33 oil fuel tank
34 hammock store
35 28cm magazine, powder
36 28cm magazine, shells
37 crypto office
38 cabin for station officer
39 artillery store
40 ammunition store
41 28cm shell room and transfer station turret C
42 engine room store
43 fresh water tank
44 trim tank
45 captain's office
46 chief engineer officer's cabin
47 teleprinter
48 admin office
49 cabin for admiral staff officer
50 reserve dressing station/seamen's sleeping room
51 10.5cm magazine
52 aft artillery plotting office
53 aft AA plotting office
54 aft artillery amplification room
55 aft artillery reserve switchboard
56 central gun training installation
57 aft AC switchboard
58 lamp store
59 washing water tank
60 hot washing water tank
61 oil fuel transfer pump room
62 leakage pump room
63 cabin
64 cabin for ship's admin officer
65 engineer NCO's launderette
66 post office store
67 cabin for admiral staff officer
68 engineering workshop
69 electrical spare parts storeroom
70 reserve tank
71 turbo power plant
72 evaporation room No 1
73 turbine room No 1
74 cabin for 2 officers
75 cabin for 2 first lieutenants
76 pantry
77 ensign's launderette
78 machinery store room No 1
79 electrical engineering workshop
80 lubrication oil collection tank
81 transfer room
82 15cm magazine for shells, illumination shells and powder
83 cable trunks
84 feed tanks
85 lubrication oil collection tank
86 reserve damage control centre
87 gyro compass room
88 machinery control centre
89 cooling machines
90 small arms store
91 reserve combat commcen
92 lubrication oil tank
93 aircraft hangar
94 wardroom
95 cabin for 3 NCOs
96 ensign's workroom
97 cabin for 1 steward and 1 printer
98 electrical engineering workshop No 2
99 aft BÜ-workshop
100 compressed air pump room
101 turbine room No 2
102 turbine room No 3
103 polluted oil tank
104 evaporation pump room
105 oily bilge water
106 wardroom pantry
107 conference room
108 engineer NCO's WC
109 artillery admin office
110 wardroom galley
111 potato store
112 admiral's and captain's galley
113 engineer NCO's deck
114 evaporation room
115 auxiliary machinery room No 1
116 boiler room No 1
117 power plant No 2
118 power control centre No 2
119 feed tank
120 oil fuel bunker control
121 feed tank, oil fuel reserve tank
122 shelter for ammunition purveyors
123 AA fire control switchboard
124 engineer NCO's pantry
125 engineer seamen's deck
126 night WC
127 forge
128 welding shop
129 aircraft ammunition
130 radio transmission room
131 seamen's bathroom
132 AA fire control switchboard
133 boiler room No 2
134 power plant No 3
135 power control centre No 3
136 evaporation room No 3
137 auxiliary machinery room No 2
138 hot water purification installation
139 boiler room No 3
140 cabin for 2 officers of the watch
141 cabin for 2 lieutenants
142 -
143 cabin for 3 lieutenants
144 cabin for chief petty officer
145 officer's showers
146 cabin for catering SNCO and carpenter SNCO
147 cabin for provost SNCO
148 artillery store
149 boom defence gear
150 bosun's cabin
151 cabin for 2 SNCOs
152 ensign's pantry
153 damage control switchover position No 2
154 auxiliary machinery room No 3
155 power plant No 4 (switchover position)
156 power control centre No 4
157 cabin for navigation officer
158 cabin for 1 officer
159 cabin for artillery officer
160 pharmacy
161 cabin for 2 medical SNCOs
162 oil fuel transfer station
163 artillery workshop
164 electrical store
165 electrical store
166 power plant No 5
167 auxiliary machinery room No 3
168 diesel tank
169 control centre
170 cabin for meteorologists
171 radio workshop
172 hospital WC
173 ante-room
174 launderette
175 bathroom
176 shelter
177 cabin for 5 tailors
178 pumpmaster's workshop
179 store room
180 artillery landing party store room
181 gas protection store room
182 hosepipe store
183 alternator for radio receiver
184 radio receiver
185 dressing station
186 fore artillery reserve switchboard
187 fore artillery switchboard
188 fore artillery
189 fore AA switchboard
190 3.7cm magazine
191 central gun training installation
192 fore AC switchboard
193 bosun's store room

PLAN 07

1 NCO's deck
2 sailmaker's workshop
3 detention cells
4 bosun's store
5 rope store
6 reserve oil fuel tanks
7 seamen's heads
8 NCO's WC
9 sail store
10 trim tank
11 chart house
12 surgeon
13 cabin for 1 officer
14 hospital
15 shoemaker
16 seamen's deck and dressing station
17 control centre
18 fore artillery plotting office
19 instruments- and charts store
20 blank ammunition store
21 air cooler for artillery control centre
22 signalling ammunition
23 fore artillery amplification room
24 gyro compass room
25 leakage pump room
26 admin officer's store
27 fore AA plotting office
28 bread store
29 hosepipe store
30 clothing store
31 canteen store
32 seamen's deck
33 oil fuel tank
34 artillery store
35 28cm powder magazine
36 cool room
37 fireworker's store
38 beer store
39 washing water tanks
40 fresh water tanks
42 NCO's sleeping room
43 28cm shell room and transfer station, turret A
125 engineer NCO's deck
190 3.7cm magazine

PLAN 10

1 10.5m base rangefinder on 28cm turret A (later removed, openings sealed)
2 10.5m base rangefinder on 28cm turret B
3 10.5m base rangefinder on 28cm turret B
4 fore conning tower with 7m base rangefinder
5 foretop with 10.5m base rangefinder and radar
6 aft conning tower with 10.5m base rangefinder and radar
7 torpedo tubes, port and starboard (mounted in Brest)
8 15cm turrets, twin mountings, starboard I and IV, port I and IV
9 15cm turrets, single mountings, starboard II and III, port II and III
10 10.5cm AA guns, twin mountings
11 3.7cm AA guns, twin mountings
12 hangar
13 2cm AA guns, single mountings
14 AA director control towers
15 reserve propellers
16 main mast
17 28cm turrets A, B and C
18 searchlight
19 funnel
20 bridge wings, starboard and port
21 breakwater
22 catapult
23 cranes, starboard and port
24 2cm AA guns, quadruple mountings (guns on 15cm turrets starboard I and port I fitted in Brest, guns on funnel platform fitted in 1941, guns at hangar side fitted in Brest)
25 radar aerial FuMO 27 on aft conning tower (fitted in 1941)
26 boat cranes, starboard and port

PLAN 11

This description of the ship's rig only contains those parts of the rig which could clearly be identified and read on the original plans.

rig

1 flag halyard
2 stay for anchor ball
3 line
4 lines for aerials
5 lifts for wishbones
6 foot ropes for wishbones
7 spring strops for wishbones
8 connecting ropes for wishbones
9 lines for wishbones
10 brace lines for wishbones
11 lines for night signalling device
12 halyard for night signalling device
13 hauling-up slip
14 wind rope for main mast
15 wind rope for aft mast
16 n/a
17 Jacob's ladder
18 n/a
19 n/a
20 lifts for aerial yard
21 top tackle for boat cranes
22 lift rope for boat cranes
23 top tackle for aircraft cranes
24 lift rope for aircraft cranes
25 n/a
26 n/a
27 line for cutter davit
28 line for cutter davit
29 man ropes for cutter davit
30 cutter falls for cutter davit
31 net gangway for cutter davit
32 lifts for boom
33 cap for boom
34 front line for boom
35 rear line for boom
36 lanyard and deadeyes for boom
37 lanyard and deadeyes for boom
38 boom stay
39 boat lines
40 boat ladder
41 lifts for stern boom
42 lift
43 lift for aft boom
44 vang
45 n/a
46 connecting line
47 lift
48 up- and down tackle
49 vang
50 ladder for boats
51 line for gangway
52 lanyard for gangway
53 lines for canvas hood
54 propeller protector lift
55 propeller protector line
56 flag staff tackle
57 quarter deck lines
58 bridge wing lines
59 n/a
60 signal flags of combat signalling station
61 warning light lines
62 aerial shroud
63 n/a
64 funnel stay

aerial arrangement

a LF-transmitting aerial, radio room A
c HF-transmitting aerial, radio room A
c HF-transmitting aerial, radio room A
d n/a
e HF-transmitting aerial, radio room B
f HF-transmitting aerial, radio room B
g LF-transmitting aerial, radio room C
h HF-transmitting aerial, radio room C
i HF-transmitting aerial, radio room C
j HF-receiving aerial, radio room A
k HF-receiving aerial, radio room A
l LF-receiving aerial, radio room A
m HF-receiving aerial, radio room A
n HF-receiving aerial, radio room B
o LF-receiving aerial, radio room B
p HF-receiving aerial, radio room C
q HF-receiving aerial, radio room C
r LF-receiving aerial, radio room C
s LF-receiving aerial, radio room C
t receiving aerial store room
u auxiliary aerial for tactical direction finder, radio room A
v auxiliary aerial for navigation device, charthouse
w aerial meteorological station
x aerial meteorological station
y broadcast receiving aerial, radio room A
z UHF-transmitting aerial, UHF-room
ä 40/70 W aerial (reserve), UHF-room
ö broadcast receiving aerial, admiral's cabin
ü cross-loop aerial for navigation device in charthouse

PLAN 12

1 hangar (after reconstruction)
2 2cm AA gun quadruple mountings, starboard and port (fitted in Brest)
3 cranes starboard and port
4 turbine room, port
5 turbine room, starboard
6 torpedo tubes, starboard and port (fitted in Brest)
7 boiler room No 1
8 boiler room No 2
9 boiler room No 3
10 platform for 2cm AA gun quadruple mountings on 15cm turrets starboard I and port I (fitted in Brest)
11 10.5cm AA guns twin mountings
12 2cm AA gun quadruple mounting on funnel platform
13 10.5m base rangefinder foretop
14 observation platform foretop (fitted in Brest)

rig

1 flag halyard
2 stay for anchor ball
3 line
4 lines for aerials
7 spring strops for wishbones
8 connecting ropes for wishbones
9 lines for wishbones
61 warning light lines
62 aerial shroud

aerial arrangement

a LF-transmitting aerial, radio room A
c HF-transmitting aerial, radio room A
f HF-transmitting aerial, radio room B
g LF-transmitting aerial, radio room B
h HF-transmitting aerial, radio room C
i HF-transmitting aerial, radio room C
j HF-receiving aerial, radio room A
k LF-receiving aerial, radio room A
l LF-receiving aerial, radio room A
m HF-receiving aerial, radio room B
n HF-receiving aerial, radio room B
o LF-receiving aerial, radio room B
p HF-receiving aerial, radio room C
q HF-receiving aerial, radio room C
t receiving aerial store room
z UK-transmitting aerial
ä 40/70 W aerial (reserve), UK-room
ü cross-loop aerial for navigation device in charthouse

Bibliography

Aßmann, Kurt, *Deutsche Seestrategie in zwei Weltkriegen* (Heidelberg, 1957)v

Bekker, Cajus, *Augen durch Nacht und Nebel* (Oldenburg, 1978)

Bennett, Geoffrey, *Seeschlachten im 2 Weltkrieg* (Koblenz/Bonn, 1981)

Bensel, Rolf, *Die deutsche Flottenpolitik von 1933-1939* (Berlin, 1958)

Bidlingmaier, Gerhard, *Einsatz der schweren Kriegsmarineeinheiten im ozeanischen Zufuhrkrieg* (Neckargemünd, 1969)

Bräckow, Werner, *Die Geschichte des deutschen Marine-Ingenieur Offizierskorps* (Oldenburg, 1974)

Bredemeier, Heinrich, *Schlachtschiff Scharnhorst* (Herford, 1978)

Breyer, Siegfried, *Großkampfschiffe 1905-1970*, Vol 1 'Großbritannien und Deutschland' (München, 1977)

Breyer, Siegfried, *Großkampfschiffe 1905-1970*, 2nd print (Koblenz, 1990)

Breyer, Siegfried, *Schlachtschiffe und Schlachtkreuzer 1905-1970* (München, 1970)

Breyer, Siegfried, *Schlachtschiff Gneisenau* (Friedberg, 1987) (Marinearsenal)

Breyer, Siegfried, *Schlachtschiff Scharnhorst* (Friedberg, 1987) (Marinearsenal)

Breyer, Siegfried/Koop, Gerhard, *Von der Emden zur Tirpitz*, Vol 1 (München, 1982)

Breyer, Siegfried/Koop, Gerhard, *Die deutsche Kriegsmarine 1939 - 1945*, Vols 4 and 5 (Friedberg, 1988, 1989)

Busch, Fritz Otto, *Tragödie am Nordkap. Untergang des Schlachtschiffes Scharnhorst* (Hannover, 1952)

Churchill, Winston S, *Der Zweite Weltkrieg* (Bern, 1949)

Conway's All the World's Fighting Ships, 1922 - 1946 (London, 1980)

Diwald, Helmut, *Der Kampf um die Weltmeere* (München/Zürich, 1980)

Dönitz, Karl, *Zehn Jahre und zwanzig Tage. Erinnerungen 1939-1945*, 9th print (Koblenz, 1985)

Dülffer, Jost, *Weimar, Hitler und die Marine* (Düsseldorf, 1972)

Dulin/Garzke, *Battleships*, Vol 3 (Annapolis, 1986)

Ewers, H, *Kriegsschiffbau* (Berlin, 1943)

Friedmann, Norman, *Battleships* (London, 1978)

Gießler, Helmuth, *Der Marine-Nachrichten- und -Ortungsdienst* (München, 1971)

Gröner, Erich, *Die deutschen Kriegsschiffe 1815-1945*, Vol 1, 2nd print (Koblenz, 1989)

Hadeler, Wilhelm, *Kriegsschiffbau* (Darmstadt, 1968)

Handbuch zur deutschen Militärgeschichte 1648-1939, Vol 4, section VIII 'Deutsche Marinegeschichte der Neuzeit' (Militärgeschichtliches Forschungsamt, München, 1979)

Hildebrand, Hans H/Stöhr, Albert/Steimnetz, Hans-Otto, *Die deutschen Kriegsschiffe*, Biographien, Vols 2 and 5 (Herford, 1980 and 1982)

Hitlers Weisungen für die Kriegführung 1939-1945, 2nd print (Walther Hubatsch, Koblenz, 1983)

Hubatsch, Walther, *'Weserübung' Die deutsche Besetzung von Dänemark und Norwegen 1940*, 2nd print (Göttingen, 1960)

Johannesson, Rolf, *Offizier in kritischer Zeit* (Herford, 1989)

Jung, Dieter/Abendroth, Arno/Kelling, Norbert, *Anstriche und Tarnanstriche der Kriegsmarine* (München, 1977)

Kähler, Wolfgang, *Schlachtschiff Gneisenau* (Herford, 1979)

Koop, Gerhard/Galle, Kurt/Klein, Fritz, *Von der Kaiserlichen Werft zum Marinearsenal. Wilhelmshaven als Zentrum der Marinetechnik seit 1870* (München, 1982)

Koop, Gerhard/Mulitze, Erich, *Die Marine in Wilhelmshaven* (Koblenz, 1987)

Vorträge des Oberbefehlshabers der Kriegsmarine vor Hitler1939-1945 (Gerhard Wagner, München, 1972)

Lewin, Ronald, *Entschied ULTRA den Krieg? Alliierte Funkauf-klärung im 2 Weltkrieg* (Koblenz/Bonn, 1981)

Lochner, R K, *Als das Eis brach* (München, 1983)

Lohmann, Walter/Hildebrand Hans H, *Die deutsche Kriegsmarine1939-1945 Gliederung, Organisation, Stellenbesetzung*, 3 vols (Bad Nauheim, 1956-1964)

Pemsel, Helmut, *Seeherrschaft: Eine maritime Weltgeschichte von den Anfängen der Seefahrt bis zur Gegenwart*, 2 vols (Koblenz, 1985)

Pemsel, Helmut, *Biographisches Lexikon zur Seekriegsgeschichte* (Koblenz, 1985)

Peter, K H, *Schlachtschiff Scharhnorst: Kampf und Untergang*, 2nd print (Frankfurt aM, 1959)

Potter, Elmer B/Nimitz, Chester W/Rohwer, Jürgen, *Seemacht: Eine Seekriegsgeschichte von der Antike bis zur Gegenwart* (München, 1974)

Potter, JD, *'Durchbruch' Die Heimkehr der Schlachtschiffe Scharnhorst und Gneisenau* (Wien/Hamburg, 1970)

Raeder, Erich, *Mein Leben*, 2 vols (Tübingen, 1956/57)

Raven, Alan/Roberts, John, *Die britischen Schlachtschiffe des Zweiten Weltkrieges*, 3 vols (München, 1980/81)

Robertson, T, *Sie wagten das Äußerste: Der abenteuerliche Durch-bruch deutscher Schlachtschiffe durch den Ärmelkanal* (Stuttgart, 1958)

Rohwer, Jürgen/Hümmelchen, Gerhard, *Chronik des Seekrieges1939-1945* (Oldenburg/Hamburg, 1968)

Salewski, Michael, *Die deutsche Seekriegsleitung 1935-1945*, 3 vols (Frankfurt aM/München, 1970-1975)

Schmalenbach, Paul, *Die Geschichte der deutschen Schiffsartillerie* (Herford, 1968)

Whitley, *German Capital Ships of World War II* (London, 1989)

Periodicals

Jahrbuch der Schiffbautechnischen Gesellschaft (numerous vols)
Leinen los/Atlantische Welt/Flotte/Marine (numerous vols)
Marineforum (numerous vols)
Marine-Rundschau (numerous vols)
Schiffbau (numerous vols)
Truppenpraxis (numerous vols)
Warship
Newspapers, magazines (numerous vols)

Sources and unpublished documents

Author's archives

Dipl -Ing Többicke (Marineoberbaurat z.Wv.) *Die Panzerung der deutschen Kriegsschiffe*

Burkhardt, Hermann, (Marineoberbaudirektor a.D.) *Die Entwicklung des Schiffbaumaterials der Deutschen Kriegsmarine*

Burkhardt, Hermann, *Die Entwicklung des Unterwasserschutzes in der Deutschen Kriegsmarine*

Burkhardt, Hermann, *Der Einfluß des Kriegsschiffbaues auf die Entwicklung der Technik*

Pfitzmann, *Schiffsansprengungen und Kriegserfahrungen*

Cordes, Ludwig, (Ministerialdirigent a.D.), Diverse correspondence

Cordes, Ludwig, 'Principles of Design of Naval Gunmountings used in German Practice' for the Historial Division (1948/50)

Bundesarchiv-Militärarchiv, Freiburg i Br
III M 300/5 KTB Flotte
IR M 309/1 KTB *Gneisenau*
IR M 310/2 KTB *Scharnhorst*
IR M 300/7 KTB Flotte

OKM *Unterlagen und Richtlinien zur Bestimmung der Hauptkampfentfernungen und der Geschoßwahl* (1940)

Illustration acknowledgements

Kriegsmarinewerft Wilhelmshaven (3)
Urbahns (1)
Deutsche Werke Kiel (2)
Küstenmuseum Wilhelmshaven (1)
PK/Koop collection (63)

Drawings of the ship's crests by Franz Mrva
Line drawings and plans by Klaus-Peter Schmolke